Colleen Dewhurst

Photograph of Colleen Dewhurst courtesy of the Billy Rose Theatre Collection, The New York Public Library for the Performing Arts, Astor, Lenox and Tilden Foundations.

Colleen Dewhurst

A Bio-Bibliography

Barbara Lee Horn

Bio-Bibliographies in the Performing Arts,
Number 37

Greenwood Press
Westport, Connecticut • London

Library of Congress Cataloging-in-Publication Data

Horn, Barbara Lee.
   Colleen Dewhurst : a bio-bibliography / Barbara Lee Horn.
      p.   cm.—(Bio-bibliographies in the performing arts, ISSN
   0892-5550 ; no. 37)
   Includes index.
   ISBN 0-313-28733-3 (alk. paper)
      1. Dewhurst, Colleen.   2. Dewhurst, Colleen—Bibliography.
   3. Actors—United States—Biography.   I. Title.   II. Series.
   PN2287.D462H6   1993
   792'.028'092—dc20
   [B]   92-31652

British Library Cataloguing in Publication Data is available.

Library of Congress Catalog Card Number: 92-31652
ISBN: 0-313-28733-3
ISSN: 0892-5550

First published in 1993

Greenwood Press, 88 Post Road West, Westport, CT 06881
An imprint of Greenwood Publishing Group, Inc.

Printed in the United States of America

∞™

The paper used in this book complies with the
Permanent Paper Standard issued by the National
Information Standards Organization (Z39.48-1984).

10 9 8 7 6 5 4 3 2 1

This book is for my grandson,
Devin Michael Boyle

"The theatre has always meant freedom to me, and freedom has always been my aim. Remember, I once wanted to fly, to be free of everything and everybody. Somehow I get that feeling when I act on a stage. "

Colleen Dewhurst

"Sure she's like an earth mother, but in real life she's not to be let out without a keeper. She's a pushover, a pussycat. She's the madonna of the birds with broken wings."

Maureen Stapleton

Contents

Preface

Jo Van Fleet visited her backstage during <u>Moon for the Misbegotten</u>, her first Broadway hit. "You're a very lucky girl, you've found your playwright," she said.[1] The lucky girl was Colleen Dewhurst; the playwright, Eugene O'Neill. And no other actress had ever been so identified with his women. "Fortunate the day I started with O'Neill, " Dewhurst later acknowledged.[2] "I am grateful such a man was writing within the time span of my life."[3]

The purpose of this study is to document the career of one of America's foremost actresses, whose career was most closedly identified with the works of Eugene O'Neill. Her seminal characterizations in the plays of O'Neill highlighted a career on stage, screen, and in television that spanned forty years and earned her two Tony Awards and four Emmys. Colleen Dewhurst was an imposing presence both in person and on stage, as even a cursory examination of this book reveals.

This study is divided into five sections. The first is a chronology of the major events in the life of Dewhurst. This is followed by a biographical sketch, which explores the public and, to a lesser degree, the private side, focusing on her career and her accomplishments. The next section is a comprehensive chronological catalogue of stage, film, and television productions, in which she appeared or directed. Data for theatre productions includes production and cast credits, opening dates and runs; and synopses of plays, other than the classics, which are of common knowledge. Opening night reviews of the major New York theater critics are listed. Data for feature film productions includes production and cast credits, country of origin, year of distribution, and synopses of teleplays. Only reviews that pertain to Dewhurst's performances are listed. Data for films made for television includes production and cast credits, network and air dates, synopses, and, again, reviews that pertain to Dewhurst's performance. The production section also includes a list of television episodes, series, and specials, in which she appeared.

The fourth section comprises a selective annotated bibliography devoted to books, periodicals, and newspaper articles written about

Dewhurst and her productions. It is presented in chronological order and reads like a narrative.

An appendix lists Dewhurst's theatre and television awards.

For convenience in indexing, items in the various credits and bibliographical sections have been enumerated and prefixed with alphabetical entry codes. The prefix "P" refers to productions. The prefix "A" refers to books, periodical or newspaper articles written about Dewhurst.

For their friendly cooperation, I wish to thank the archival staff of the Billy Rose Theatre Collection of the New York Public Library of the Performing Arts at Lincoln Center

I want to thank Marilyn Brownstein of Greenwood Press for her assistance, encouragement, and advice, for which I am extremely grateful. My thanks go also to Donna Geffner and St. John's University for giving me the time to do my research and writing.

---

[1] Rebecca Morehouse, "A Theatregoer's Notebook: Homage to O'Neill," Playbill 88(June 1988), n.p. (Clippings, Theatre Collection, New York Public Library.)

[2] John Corry, "Theater: A New Test for Colleen Dewhurst," The New York Times (September 26, 1982): III, 4.

[3] Morehouse.

Chronology

1924   Born on June 3, 1924, in Montreal, Canada, the only child of Mr. & Mrs. Fred Dewhurst.

1938   Her parents divorce.

1943   Portrays Olivia in <u>As You Like It</u> in her senior year at a Milwaukee high school.

1944   Attends Milwaukee Downer College for Young Ladies for one year.

1945   Works as a dental receptionist in Gary, Indiana.

1946   Comes to New York and enrolls in the American Academy of Dramatic Arts.

        Performs the role of Julia Cavendish in theAmerican Academy production of <u>The Royal Family</u> on October 15.

1947   Marries James Vickery.

1948   Completes her training at the American Academy of Dramatic Arts.

        Makes her debut in a stock company production of <u>Personal Appearance</u> in Knoxville, Tennessee.

        Takes private acting classes with Joseph Kramm and Joseph Anthony of the American Theatre Wing.

1952   Makes her first Broadway appearance as a dancer in
        O'Neill's Desire Under the Elms.
        Studies with Harold Clurman.

        Comes to the attention of Joseph Papp.

1954   Performs in a reading, An Evening With Shakespeare and
        Marlow, in a Papp workshop at the Emmanuel Presbyterian
        Church.

1956   Appears on Broadway in January as a Turkish Concubine
        and a Virgin of Memphis in Tamburlaine the Great.

        Plays Kate in Shakespeare's The Taming of the Shrew in
        Papp's first summer series in the park at the East River
        Amphitheatre. Atkinson of The New York Times praises her
        performance in his review.

        Heads the cast in a revival of Alexander Dumas's Camille at
        the Off-Broadway Cherry Lane Theatre in September.

        Plays the lead in Jean Cocteau's The Eagle Has Two Heads
        at the Actors Playhouse in December.

        Wins her first Obie for her performances in The Eagle Has
        Two Heads and The Taming of the Shrew.

1958   Appears in the Greenwich Village Circle in the Square
        production of Edwin Justus Mayer's Children of Darkness
        with George C. Scott. The production is staged by Jose
        Quintero, who becomes her director for many O'Neill roles.

        Portrays Josie, directed by Quintero, in A Moon For the
        Misbegotten at the Spoleto Festival in Italy.

1959   Plays Cleopatra to Scott's Antony for Papp in Shakespeare's
        Antony and Cleopatra at the Heckscher Theatre.

1960   Appears in her first major Broadway role as Caesonia, the
        mistress of the despotic emperor, in Albert Camus's Caligula.
        Divorces Vickery and marries George C. Scott.

1961   Wins her first Tony Award as best featured actress for her
        portrayal of a suddenly widowed young mother in Tad

Mosel's <u>All the Way Home</u>. Selected also for the Lola D'Annunzio Award.

1962   Directed by Quintero in Alice Cannon's comedy <u>Great Day in the Morning</u>.

1963   Returns to the Circle in the Square and to O'Neill's <u>Desire Under the Elms</u> as Abbie Putnam in a critically praised production directed by Quintero. Wins her second Obie.

Plays Gertrude to James Earl Jones's Claudius and Stacy Keach's Hamlet in the New York Shakespeare Festival production that opens the new Delacorte Theatre in Central Park.

Directed by Edward Albee in Carson McCullers' <u>Ballad of the Sad Cafe</u>.

1965   Tours during the summer as Martha in Albee's <u>Who's Afraid of Virginia Woolf?</u>

1967   Remarries Scott, whom she divorced in 1963.

1969   Appears Off-Broadway as Hester in Athol Fugard's <u>Hello and Goodbye</u> and wins a Drama Desk Award for her performance.

1970   Plays Shen Teh in <u>The Good Woman of Setzuan</u> at the Vivian Beaumont at Lincoln Center.

1971   Portrays Amelia in Albee's <u>All Over</u>.

1972   Divorces Scott for the second time on February 2, 1972.

Appears as Gertrude in the New York Shakespeare Festival production of <u>Hamlet</u> at the Delacorte Theatre in the Central Park.

Receives an honorary doctorate in fine arts from Lawrence University.

1973   Nominated for a Tony award for her performance as Christine in O'Neill's <u>Mourning Becomes Electra</u>.

1974   Wins a Tony award and a Drama Desk award for her
            portrayal of Josie in <u>Moon for the Misbegotten</u>. The
            production, which is her first and only Broadway success, is
            staged by Quintero and co-stars Jason Robards.

1977   Opens to standing ovations in a revival of Albee's <u>Who's</u>
            <u>Afraid of Virginia Woolf?</u>, in which she had toured in the
            summer of 1965.

1981   Makes her directorial debut with <u>Ned and Jack</u> at the Hudson
            Guild Theatre.

1982   Performs in the role of the Queen in <u>The Queen and the</u>
            <u>Rebels</u>, a Circle in the Square production presented at the
            Plymouth Theatre.

            Protests in an unsuccessful fight to save the Helen Hayes,
            Morosco, and Bijou Theatres on Broadway.

1983   Displays her talent for comedy in a cameo role in Moss Hart
            and George S. Kaufman's <u>You Can't Take It With You</u>.

1985   Elected President of Actors' Equity. Holds office for two
            three-years terms; declines to run for a third.

1986   Wins an Emmy award for her portrayal of Barbara Petherton
            in the television mini series, <u>Between Two Women</u>.

1987   Portrays Carlotta Monterey O'Neill in <u>My Gene</u>, a one-
            woman play by Barbara Gelb at the New York Shakespeare
            Festival.

1988   Performs as Mary Tyrone in <u>Long Day's Journey Into Night</u>
            and Essie Miller in <u>Ah, Wilderness!</u> in repertory for New
            York International Festival of the Arts.

1989   Receives an Emmy for her performance (with Candice
            Bergen) in the television comedy series, <u>Murphy Brown</u>; and
            another for her performance in the made-for-television-film
            <u>Those She Left Behind</u>.

1991   Makes her last appearance in the film, <u>Termini Station</u>.

Dies of cancer at the age of sixty-seven on August 22.

Receives her fourth Emmy award, again for her portrayal of the mother in the <u>Murphy Brown</u> series, three days after her death.

Biography

Every marquee on Broadway darkened for several minutes on the evening following her passing. She was one of America's foremost actresses and one of the most honored and admired performers of her generation. Colleen Dewhurst died of cancer at the age of sixty-seven on August 22, 1991, at her home in South Salem Village, New York.

In a two-hour "Remembrance" one month later nearly 1,300 friends, colleagues, and admirers gathered at the Martin Beck Theatre on Broadway. The impressive but unassuming actress, known for her distinctive husky voice--aggravated by cigarettes--was remembered for the special dimension she brought to the plays of Eugene O'Neill. She was remembered for her regal stature, her mature sexuality, her folksy earthiness, her quick sense of humor; and, most of all, she was remembered for her irrepressible laughter. "I can't shake it out of my ears," said actor Roscoe Lee Browne; it was an "engulfing, encompassing laugh," declared playwright Edward Albee; a laugh that built from sensual baritone to shy, girlish giggle," contributed actor Arvin Brown; "intoxicating," "Olympian," "therapeutic," added others.[1]

"I depended on her for stillness," said Arvin Brown. "I never knew another like it, either in performance . . . or in private conversation." Recounting a long silent moment on stage which Dewhurst concluded with the quiet reach of an arm, he added that her gesture "never dissipated an emotion; it summarized it, always."[2]

Dewhurst's seminal characterizations in the plays of Eugene O'Neill highlighted a forty-year career on stage, screen, and television that brought her honors and praise in every medium. But it was as a stage actress--and particularly as an interpreter without equal of O'Neill's tragic women--that her impact was most deeply felt. In 1974, she won a Tony Award for her portrayal of Josie Hogan in the acclaimed revival of A Moon for the Misbegotten (P28). She was nominated for a Tony in 1973 for her performance as Christine in Mourning Becomes Electra (P26) in which she won recognition as a preeminent tragic actress; and she won an Obie Award early in her career as Abbie Putnam in Desire Under the Elms (P2) in 1952. Her most recent appearances were on Broadway in 1988 as Mary Tyrone in Long Day's Journey Into Night (P42) and as Essie Miller in Ah, Wilderness! (P41)--the former being O'Neill's anguished family portrait, the latter its comedic mirror image--in a marathon repertory performance of a kind rarely seen on Broadway. In the late 1980s she toured widely in My Gene (P40), a monodrama written by O'Neill's biographer Barbara Gelb about the playwright's wife Carlotta. The one-woman play had originated at Joseph Papp's Public Theater the year before.

As a fledgling actress during the early 1950s, she did a scene from Desire Under the Elms for acting coach Joe Anthony at the Theatre Wing. Even though she was too young for the part, she knew that O'Neill was her writer.[3] Explaining her special attraction for his women, Dewhurst later said: "I love the O'Neill women. They move from the groin rather than the brain. To play O'Neill you have to be big. You can't sit around and play little moments of sadness or sweetness."[4]

Born in Canada

Dewhurst was born in Montreal, Canada, on June 3, 1924. Of Irish-Scotch-English ancestry, she was the only child. Her father, Fred Dewhurst, a professional hockey and football player (who later became a salesman for a lighting concern), brought her up as an athlete and frequently took her to sporting events with him.[5] Her mother was "a petite beauty" who descended from a line of Ulster Irish; she became a Christian Science practitioner after a "swinging life," although at first she thought it was "mumbo jumbo."[6] Her grandfather was "shot in the leg leading an Orangeman's parade."[7]

Her parents moved to Boston and later to Milwaukee. In several interviews, Dewhurst remembered her childhood as a particularly happy period.[8] She was very thin as a child and recalls her father's insisting that she eat. She had tuberculin glands of the neck, which resulted in a series of surgeries that left visible scars and a "whisky" voice quality.[9] As a disguise, she wore a handkerchief around her neck--until the day that Mrs. Dewhurst joined the Christian Science Church. Her mother "took off the hanky and threw it away. No explanation was ever given. I remember because it was so super."[10]

Her parents divorced when she was twelve. After that, it was mother and daughter alone. Dewhurst spoke of her mother as "a woman ahead of her time, a compassionate woman of great humor and incredible intellect."[11] She was "great fun...we were very close."[12]

Once she left home, Dewhurst no longer practiced the faith of her mother's choice--she was a Lucky Strike chain-smoker and enjoyed white wine--yet she insisted that "everything I like about myself comes from the religion, and when I get in a bad bind, my mind goes back to it."[13]

Interest in Theatre Is Kindled

She was not interested in becoming an actress as a youngster. In her words:

Being very much of a tomboy, I wanted to be an aviatrix. Since I was also interested in writing, my mother said that, if I would go to college for two years, she would let me take up flying. In my senior year in a Milwaukee high school--one of fifteen schools I went to from the time we moved down from Montreal--all that changed.[14]

An English teacher, who was casting according to the way characters should look, selected Dewhurst for the part of Olivia in As You Like It. Her first performance, as it happened, was in a Shakespeare play; and several years later her big break would come from playing Kate in The Taming of the Shrew (P6). Her classroom experience, she confided, was agony; and she endured only because it was a requirement for a speech course. All Dewhurst remembered of the show was that, "When it came time to itemize the beautiful qualities of my features, my veil got caught, and it brought the house down."[15]

As a freshman at Milwaukee Downer College for Young Ladies, Dewhurst acted in a skit she had written and directed for a freshman class, only because she was impatient with the female lead's interpretation.[16] At that time her declared interest in journalism waned with the realization that she wanted to be an actress.

Mrs. Dewhurst was none too pleased when Colleen announced her wish to go to New York to study acting. She asserted that permission would be granted only after observing her daughter in performance.[17]

In a play about Louis Pasteur, written by one of her friends, Dewhurst played the character who pleads for the serum before it has been perfected. Nothing went smoothly. After the performance that night, mother and daughter sat in the still of their darkened living room. Expecting the worst, Mrs. Dewhurst broke the silence with words of encouragement.[18]

With only another year left to complete the two year program at Downer, Dewhurst dropped out. The president of the college had written a note criticizing her lack of academic seriousness. Mrs. Dewhurst, in complete agreement, decided that a year's indoctrination in earning a living might be a more sobering educational experience. So off Colleen went to Gary, Indiana--she had a friend there--where she sought employment unsuccessfully in a defense factory. Her Canadian birth prevented her from obtaining war related work. She did become a U.S. citizen later on. One day, while operating an elevator and complaining about a toothache, a dentist, who happened to be in the car, offered her a position as his dental receptionist.[19]

At the end of her year's commitment to work--as if she were counting off the days--Dewhurst moved to New York City. In 1946 she enrolled in the American Academy of Dramatic Arts, never to miss a day of classes. A year later, while at the Academy, she married James Vickery, a fellow student actor, at the Little Church Around the Corner.[20] The couple lived together for twelve years in a series of cold-water flats, supporting themselves with odd jobs that would give them time to look for acting positions. Jim worked in drugstores; Colleen as a receptionist, a telephone operator, and an exercise instructor for ladies at a local gym.[21]

Early Stage Career: Summer Stock and Bit Parts in New York

After graduating from the Academy, Dewhurst made her debut in the stock company production of Personal Appearance in Knoxville, Tennessee. She played a villainess who attempts to seduce a young boy. In the next production (Dewhurst never mentions the title of the play), she was a wisecracking woman.[22]   Many sources, however, consider her first professional performance to be the one she gave in the role of Julia Cavendish in The American Academy production of The Royal Family (P1) on October 15, 1946, which was staged at the Carnegie Lyceum.[23] She continued to studying acting, taking private classes with Joseph Kramm and Joseph Anthony of the American Theatre Wing. And for the first ten years of her career, ten weeks of summer stock became a way of life.

In 1952, Dewhurst made her first Broadway appearance in a very small role as a dancer in a revival of O'Neill's Desire Under the Elms. She had been studying with the production's director, Harold Clurman, and continued when the show closed. It was Clurman who introduced her to the great souls of Shakespeare's characters. He gave her scenes to prepare from the classics. After all the "realistic, earthbound, and kitcheny" roles she'd played, she thought "What is this?"[24]

Joseph Papp: Her First Break

Following a casual preparation of the part of Constance in King John for one of Clurman's workshop classes, Dewhurst received a telephone call from Joseph Papp. Peggy Bennion, Papp's wife, was also a member of the acting group; excited by the Constance portrayal, she told her husband about Dewhurst. At the time, Papp was in the initial stages of organizing his Shakespearean Workshop--later to become the New York Shakespeare Festival--and presenting scenes at the Emmanuel Presbyterian Church on the lower East Side of New York. Papp told Dewhurst that he wanted her to play Juliet. "Oh, Mr. Papp," Dewhurst (five-eight and big-boned) responded on the telephone, "you haven't seen me yet. I couldn't play Juliet when I was twelve."[25] She hung up. Papp persisted. He called again, finally enticing her to join his dedicated group, which included J. D. Cannon and Roscoe Browne. In 1954, she participated in a workshop reading, An Evening with Shakespeare and Marlow (P3). She was to become a Papp regular.

Cannon, who had known Dewhurst from their days at the American Academy, suggested that she be cast as Kate in The Taming of the Shrew, the second play of Papp's first summer series in the park in 1956. Stuart Vaughan, who directed the production, remembered her, as "a vigorous, truthful, and imaginative actress, with power, fire and inventiveness."[26] She was seen by Brooks Atkinson, the chief theatre critic of The New York Times, who praised her acting in print: "Colleen Dewhurst is excellent--a hard, sultry, sullen wench who becomes a radiant, soft-mannered young lady at the end."[27] With this review the public began to take notice.

Later in 1956, Dewhurst played Tamora in Papp's indoor production of Titus Andronicus (P7) opposite Papp's wife, Peggy Bennion, as Lavinia. Under his aegis again, she played Lady Macbeth in Macbeth (P11) at the Belvedere Lake Theatre in Central Park in August 1957. Writing about her performance in his column, Richard Watts, Jr., noted, "Some day a commercial manager will get around to discovering the cast's Colleen Dewhurst, an actress of true dramatic fire."[28]

Dewhurst did not appear on Broadway again until January 1956, when she played both a Turkish Concubine and a Virgin of Memphis in the Tyrone Guthrie theatre production, Tamburlaine the Great (P4).

In September 1956 she was cast as the title character in a revival of
Camille (P5) at the Off-Broadway Cherry Lane Theatre. Critics Walter
Kerr, Brooks Atkinson, and Jerry Tallmer were happy that she was
healthy, but noted that her appearance, 145 pounds and deeply tanned,
overshadowed the character who was dying of consumption.[29] In late 1956
the actress had the lead in another tragedy, Jean Cocteau's The Eagle Has
Two Heads (P8), at the Actors Playhouse. Tallmer again made reference
to the death scene, "Colleen Dewhurst dies again...Will someone please give
this girl a job so she can stop doing these things!"[30] For her portrayal of
the Queen in the revival of The Eagle Has Two Heads and her performance
in The Taming of the Shrew, Dewhurst was awarded her first Village
Voice Off-Broadway Obie award. And then, along came Tallmer's
"someone": Jose Quintero.

Enter Jose Quintero: Start of a Team

Major success began after the 1958 Greenwich Village Circle in the
Square production of Edwin Justus Mayer's Children of Darkness (P12).
The revival was staged by Quintero, who was to become her director for
many O'Neill roles. Dewhurst played Laetitia. Appearing opposite her
was another up-and-coming young performer, George C. Scott, in the role
of Lord Wainright. Kerr praised her performance: "One must stand in
honest awe of Colleen Dewhurst's sultry-mouthed, stony-eyed trollop; as
bad girls go, she is a beaut to be remembered."[31] For her portrayal of the
jailer's daughter, she won a Theatre World award.

In January 1959, Dewhurst played Cleopatra to Scott's Antony in
Shakespeare's Antony and Cleopatra (P14), a Papp production, staged at
the Heckscher Theatre. This was her second production with Scott. Their
meeting led to the divorces of their respective spouses and marriage in
1959. In time the couple bought an 18th century farmhouse in South
Salem, New York, where they planned to raise their two sons, Alexander
Scott and Campbell.

Dewhurst's first Broadway role with spoken text came in a brief
1960 production of Albert Camus's Caligula (P15). Commenting on her
portrayal of Caesonia, critic Watts thought the role made "comparatively
few demands on her remarkable talents as an actress."[32] The following
year, she won her first Tony Award, as best featured actress for her
portrayal of the widowed young mother in Tad Mosel's All the Way Home
(P16), an adaptation of James Agee's novel A Death in the Family. In this
review Watts underscored the "depth, simplicity, warmth and emotional
range" of her skilled interpretation of the young wife and mother who
grew in stature through her tragic experience.[33]

Dewhurst had not been an easy type to cast. She was not petite enough for ingenues, nor was she old enough for the character parts of contemporary dramas. Speaking of her character in All the Way Home, Dewhurst disclosed that she had felt so typed by the classics--she called herself the "revival girl"--that it was a pleasure to be playing a modern woman.[34] "Perhaps they thought I'd do as the mother and wife in this, because I was nine months pregnant when I read for it."[35]

Frances Herridge of the New York Post, who interviewed her at the time, described Dewhurst as:

A striking woman, her face and figure exude power and femininity in almost equal portions; her eyes can change from enormous passion to mirth in a split second. But on stage where she has sometimes been called the Anna Magnani of off-Broadway, she could easily overwhelm the smooth prettiness of most modern heroines.[36]

In March 1962 Dewhurst appeared on Broadway as Phoebe in Alice Cannon's comedy, Great Day in the Morning (P17). The Theatre of Michigan Company production was directed by Quintero. Her husband Scott was one of the producers.[37] Writing for The New York Times, Howard Taubman thought her "a marvelously big Phoebe . . . virtually a one woman show."[38]

In 1963, she was back at the Circle in the Square in Desire Under the Elms (P18), but this time instead of being a dancer she was a co-star with Scott and Rip Torn. The production, directed again by Quintero, won critical acclaim. Dewhurst, as Abbie Putnam, was awarded her second Obie.

Carson McCullers' Ballad of the Sad Cafe (P19) brought the actress to Broadway, also in 1963. When she heard through the theatrical grapevine that she was going to be approached by director Edward Albee to play Amelia, she got a copy of the book. Discovering that the character was a six-feet-two, cross-eyed, mannish eccentric, she wondered why Albee had her in mind and asked her husband about it. Scott smiled and said the reason might be "because I was good playing the lesbian in No Exit (P62) on TV."[39]

The role was challenging; the lines easy to learn, but difficult to feel. In all the characters she'd played, she had been able to find something of herself with which to identify. Not with Amelia--this was work.[40] After long conversations with both Albee and Scott, Dewhurst came to see the large, muscular, seemingly hard and grasping woman as handsome, not mannish. As she described the character:

> Her mother died when she was born so she was brought up by her father, with little love, almost as a boy. She was bright, but too incongruous for such things as dating boys. She was attracted to Marvin Macy (the village no-good, played by Louis Antonio) because he seemed strong and cruel enough to dominate her. But when Marvin reforms, she's confused by the change.[41]

Despite Dewhurst's coming to grips with the character and several rave reviews, the play was a box office failure.

Defending the less than ecstatic reviews of her next venture on Broadway, O'Neill's More Stately Mansions (P22) with Ingrid Bergman (1967), Dewhurst stated, "What if it is one of O'Neill's inferior plays? The fact that it's O'Neill at all should be reason enough for it to be seen."[42]

Rex Reed interviewed her the day after the opening of More Stately Mansions. By now, she had earned a reputation as one of the best actresses in America. The setting was the kitchen in her 200-year-old country farmhouse near South Salem, New York. She lunched on a bacon-cheese-and-egg sandwich, drinking Diet Pepsi from the quart bottle. The sun filtered through the window onto her rich chestnut hair, and there was no doubt that she would survive.[43]

"I tell you," she told Reed, "I never read reviews. G.C. [appellation for her husband] reads them all with glee, but I never do. I don't have to. I can tell if they're bad because the phone doesn't ring. Today I have had what I call a moderately middling phone, so I know they were pretty bad."[44]

Alexander, age 7, asked if Mommy brought any souvenirs from the opening night party. She answered, "No." Campbell, age 6, asked Mommy how it went. She answered that The New York Times liked Mommy, but not the play.[45]

In 1971, Dewhurst divorced Scott for the second time. While filming The Bible in Italy in 1963, Scott met Ava Gardner, and the first marriage to Dewhurst dissolved. Four years later, Scott and Dewhurst had remarried. In 1971, Scott met Trish Van Devere on the set of The Last Run. A year later he and Dewhurst divorced again. She kept the $750,000 house in Westchester County as part of the settlement.[46]

Her First (and Only) Broadway Success

A Moon for the Misbegotten opened at the Morosco Theatre on December 29, 1973. Dewhurst co-starred with Jason Robards in her first (and only) Broadway success. In her role as Josie Hogan, which most critics think her finest, Dewhurst seemed a natural. T.E. Kalem wrote that no actress had been big enough for the role before, "not only physically but in that generosity of heart, mind and spirit which Josie must convey."[47] According to Howard Kissel who was deeply moved by her performance:

> Colleen Dewhurst's portrayal of Josie remains a performance that taught me what theatre can be. Dewhurst has so much presence and stature her Josie could never be the plain slut she claims she is. She is a veritable Earth Mother. And because of that exalted quality she has no problem convincing us that she was not just a virgin but The Madonna.[48]

Writing in The New York Times, Clive Barnes held that Dewhurst "spoke O'Neill as if it were being spoken for the first time--and not in a theater (you always hope for that) but for the first time in a certain New England farm on a certain September night in 1923."[49]

Quintero, who staged the production, had first directed Dewhurst in A Moon for the Misbegotten (P13) for a presentation during the summer of 1958 at the Gian-Carlo Menotti Festival of Two Worlds in Spoleto, Italy. In October 1965, he had again directed her in the same role at the Buffalo Studio Arena. For her portrayal of Josie in the 1973 production, Dewhurst was awarded her second Tony.

Commenting on the Broadway production, Dewhurst said that female audiences were befuddled when they observed the bedraggled hair, old dress, and bare feet. From the minute they saw her on the stage, she knew they were thinking: that *can't* be the lead! And they always talked when "Josie" washed her face on stage. There would be a five minute discussion about whether or not she had on a special kind of makeup. "We could halt the play and wait until the first two rows are still. The last ten minutes you can forget too. They're closing purses and getting the shopping bags ready."[50]

In the same interview with Judy Stone of Playgirl, Dewhurst furthered her discoveries. The tough-talking, tenderhearted Josie failed in her attempt to seduce Jamie, the guilt-ridden alcoholic, because he preferred to view her as some redemptive Virgin Mary. His rejection put an end to her dreams and reinforced the idea that she would spend the rest of her life in the service of her father.[51] As for Jamie, there was nothing unusual about him. Everywoman had met or been with a Jamie:

> Josie is the dream woman of the American male, because in her the man finds a woman who is mommy and virginal. We talk so much about the male taking advantage of the female, but sexually the fear in the male often is that he cannot or will not be able to perform. I don't know why audiences don't pick up on Jamie's lines to Josie: 'Why did you do that if all you wanted was what the others wanted? ' And Josie's answer--so naive: 'I only wanted to give you happiness.' She's speaking from the virginal standpoint. She doesn't think of herself as taking. She is only thinking to pleasure the male. She never realizes the man is suffering from a tremendous fear of sexual failure.[52]

When the Broadway revival of Albee's Who's Afraid of Virginia Woolf? (P29) opened in 1976 to standing ovations, an elated Dewhurst confessed, "These last few years it's been like someone has cut the string on my balloon and released me. I'm just enjoying it all."[53] She was seen at the opening in the company of Ken Marsolais, one of the show's producers.[54] In Who's Afraid of Virginia Woolf?, she shared the spotlight with Ben Gazzara; Albee directed; and her portrayal of the abrasive wife won her a Tony nomination in 1977. During the summer of 1965, she had toured as Martha.

The Queen and the Rebels (1982, P35) a political drama, marked a return to Broadway after a four year hiatus. Her absence from the stage was attributed to the lack of a good play for a woman. Although she'd read hundreds of scripts since 1978, she'd found not one multidimensional female part. "There are no characters like that being written," she lodged regrets. "It's a shame. The theatre needs plays about women. I also read too many scripts with the same type of characters I've always played. I don't want a career that keeps repeating itself."[55] The fighting lead in the Ugo Betti play--about the military government's effort to execute their former queen--, suited Dewhurst well. She liked the character, she said, "because she was a survivor."[56]

"She shouldn't have to do Medea every five minutes," Scott once said, adding that he'd "like to see her in Getting Gertie's Garter, say, or Up in Mabel's Room."[57] Nevertheless, a prominence in weighty roles gave her little opportunity to display her talent in comedy. This gift was most revealing, if brief, during a six minute sequence in You Can't Take It With You (1983, P36) that stole the show. "It's a cameo role," wrote Barnes in his review, "but Miss Dewhurst, functioning as a cleanup hitter, knocks every laugh line clear out of the part."[58] Even the cast broke up one night. Dewhurst--so used to playing "heavies"-- quipped, "Gee, it's wonderful to be in a play where the audience smiles back at you when you take a curtain call."[59]

Her later stage work was highlighted by repertory roles in O'Neill's Long Day's Journey Into Night and Ah, Wilderness! (1988) presented in conjunction with the First New York International Festival of the Arts (1988); and the Public Theatre presentation of My Gene a year earlier, with which she later toured.

Early in her career, Dewhurst had appeared in other Papp productions, including Antony and Cleopatra (P20) in June 1963 without Scott (Michael Higgins played Antony). The show, which opened the new, outdoor Delacorte Theatre in Central Park, was taped by CBS and aired simultaneously on June 20, 1963. Again at the Delacorte in the summer of 1972, she played Gertrude to James Earl Jones's Claudius and Stacy Keach's Hamlet. Other Off-Broadway plays include Athol Fugard's Hello and Goodbye (P23), in which she co-starred with Martin Sheen in 1969 and won a Drama Desk Award.

Television and Film Career

Dewhurst was a prolific presence in television and film. In 1959 Quintero cast her, along with Jacqueline Brookes and Betty Miller, in the chorus of a National Educational Television production of Medea (P97), which starred Dame Judith Anderson. Her first significant television break came when the producers of the Dupont Show of the Month series did I, Don Quixote (P99) with Lee J. Cobb and Eli Wallach. She played Dulcinea and won a Sylvania Award.[60] In 1962 she was nominated for an Emmy for her performance in WNBC-TV's Focus (P101), an adaptation of Arthur Miller's novel about anti-Semitism.[61]

She was seen on television, more recently, with Candice Bergen on the Murphy Brown (P128) series for three seasons as Murphy's mother, Avery Brown, winning an Emmy Award in 1989, and another three days after her death. She also received Emmys for her roles in dramatic made-for-television-films: Between Two Women (1986, P85) and Those She Left Behind (1989, P92). She reprised Josie in A Moon for the Misbegotten (P69) for the small screen and performed in many other television adaptations from the stage, including two Arthur Miller plays, The Price (P66) for the Hallmark Hall Of Fame and The Crucible (P65). She turned up regularly on such Golden Age television dramas series as "Play of the Week," "DuPont Show Of The Month" and "U.S. Steel Hour."

Her many films include The Nun's Story(1959, P45), A Fine
Madness (1966, P47), The Cowboys (1972, P49), McQ (1974, P50) with
John Wayne, Woody Allen's Annie Hall (1977, P51), Ice Castles (1979,
P52), and Tribute(1980, P57) with Jack Lemmon. She performed in
Dying Young (1991, P60) with Julia Roberts and her son Campbell Scott,
who also acted with her in 1988 revivals of Long Day's Journey Into Night
and Ah, Wilderness!.

It was never any secret that she performed in television and film for
the money. Her heart belonged to the theatre where the money was not
important. "I'll do a TV show for thousands," she said in an interview
with Reed, "just so I can afford to work for Joe Papp in Central Park or do
something off-Broadway for $50 a week, and that's my integrity."[62]

Led Actors' Equity

In 1985 Dewhurst was elected president of Actors' Equity
Association, the 39,000-member union of stage actors and managers. She
held office for two terms and declined to run for a third term in the spring
of 1990. During her tenure, she was a tireless worker for the union, often
performing her union duties during the day and working on the stage at
night. Equity executive secretary Alan Eisenberg recalled, "She was
exceptionally incisive. She got to the heart of the matter in a nonlawyerly
way and she had wonderful instincts."[63]

Champion of Theatrical Causes

As an activist close to the hearts of actors, Dewhurst gave her time
freely to causes. She was on the board of trustees of the Actors' Fund of
America, the theatrical charity and social services agency. She served as
the chair of the fund's executive committee, which works in conjunction
with Equity Fights AIDS and Broadway Cares. She was the chair of the
advisory board of the Actors' Work Program, vice-chair of the board of
Save the Theatres, and a member of the boards of the American Council
for the Arts and the Theatre Development Fund. She was, in 1982, along
with Papp, among the most powerful and emotional protesters denouncing,
unsuccessfully as it turned out, the planned razing of the Helen Hayes,
Morosco, and Bijou Theatres on Broadway in order to make way for the
Marriott Marquis hotel.

When Equity took unpopular stands, as when it originally rejected
British actor Jonathan Pryce's petition in 1990 to re-create his Miss Saigon
role on Broadway, Dewhurst was an unshakable union backer. She was
also involved with the Partnership for the Homeless, the National Women's
Law Center, and the Lighthouse for the Blind.

Comments on Women

Although she was never officially connected with the woman's movement, she always seemed part of it--as her life seemed to identify with all the issues liberation implies. She was often approached by feminist groups, possibly because of the earth mother image that was fostered in her early career. She was sympathetic, but characteristically not hesitant to express her opinion. " I won't do anything anti-male. That whole thing is ridiculous . . . It's one of the more natural states to be with a man, but we're going to destroy everything in them that we want from them . . . I'm so bored with sexual freedom, and I'm amazed that we've managed to make sex boring. We've also managed to make the male impotent."[64]

Dewhurst very often commented on the psychology of women, as she intuited it. For example, she saw Cleopatra as a slave to the cult of external beauty--like a certain type of American woman who thinks only of her clothes, her appearance, and how to stay young forever. Cleopatra couldn't experience love as anything except flirtation. She was always getting Antony worked up into a romantic state of intoxication; but when she had to accept him as a man, without the adolescent flirtation, she went to pieces. In her late thirties, she acted like a young girl with her perception of love and marriage.[65]

This is what she had to say about the glorious-looking Ingrid Bergman. "She must have gone into shock when she saw Arthur [Hill] and me. She had us running back and forth to the dye shop to look as good as she did."[66]

As for the theatre party ladies, Dewhurst observed that whenever a show started moving into a problem area, especially where it involved women's issues, the shuffling began. If what the drama said related directly, purses began to open and close as the group fidgeted:

These women think the greatest thing in the world is to get married. They don't want to hear anything they don't understand. And what they understand is where is the home, where is the food, where is the money and where is the life insurance. So when you're into something really interesting in a play the uneasiness starts. You can sense their discomfort."[67]

This was not the way Dewhurst chose to live her life. Offering more insight on her own personality, she continued:

> I want to let myself go in life like men do. I want to live like a human being with a mind and a spirit. I want to be loved because I have that spirit. I do not want to spend my life competing with my sisters. I just want to love and be loved.[68]

Commenting on matinee audiences on another occasion, Dewhurst stated that she had often wanted to write an article about what actually happens:

> We're trying to awaken a whole group of women who have already been trained a certain way. We should be educating the mamas of those daughters we want to liberate. Then the mamas won't think marriage is the be all and end all and that not only do they have to get married but kill him after he's married to be sure that he doesn't in any way wander, and if he does . . . "[69]

The Importance of Eugene O'Neill

Reflecting on her career, Dewhurst commented, "You are not aware that it's going to end up where people hear your name and say, 'O'Neill,' but I'll just face the fact that I'm really grateful to this man. When I came to New York, I wasn't what they were looking for; I was considered too tall. The O'Neill women appeared early because Jose [Quintero] threw me into that area."[70]

As for her favorite role, it was difficult to say. It wasn't Josie, though she fully appreciated her; and she loved the lady in Desire Under the Elms. As for playwrights, her most satisfaction had come from O'Neill and Albee.[71]

The Farm: Her Eye in the Storm

She lived on a farm in South Salem, Westchester County, New York, with her companion of the last sixteen years, the Broadway producer Ken Marsolais. The thirty-five room, two-hundred-year-old farmhouse was home to eight cats, two dogs, one goat, and a parrot, a housekeeper and assorted transient and semiresidential house guests. She also had a summer home on Prince Edward Island, Canada.

She referred to the farm, which is about an hour and fifteen minute drive into the city, as her eye in the storm. "You know," she once reflected, "I'm very conscious about not leaving this house. The kids like having me around in the morning. That's why I'm so firm about coming home every evening. I find absolute life up here . . .The truth is I need it all--the kids, the play, the house--everything."[72]

Awards

Her career earned her two Tony Awards and four Emmys, but she was also most proud of the honorary doctorate in fine arts that she received in 1972 from Lawrence University, which had merged with Downer College, her alma mater.

Commendations

In his "Homage" to Dewhurst, Otis Stuart splendidly captured her contribution to the art of acting. She began in the traditional classics in roles that included Lady Macbeth, Cleopatra, and Camille, but crowned her career in the contemporary plays of Albee and, importantly, O'Neill. In her forty years onstage, as the workshops of the Group Theatre/ Actor's Studio grew to become a world force, she grew *en tandem* to embody the discoveries of American acting: the physicality, the gesture as important as speech. And these defining qualities took "epic scale in the poetry of her person, from her sheer size to her forthright sexuality to the elemental force that made Maureen Stapleton call her on stage 'the earth mother of us all.'"[73]

"You don't have to be a great person to be a great actor," said Papp, "but she happened to combine both."[74] Her death is a great loss to the American theatre and a great loss to me personally," noted George C. Scott.[75] "There was a great tenacity, a ferocity, and absolute truth about her," said Theodore Mann. "She loved and believed in the actor, in the gift a person could give to another by stepping on the stage. She always reminded me that actors on stage are our royalty."[76]

Colleen Dewhurst will long be remembered as the the earthy actress of absolute truth and passion who brought a special dimension to the plays of Eugene O'Neill. As Josie in <u>A Moon for the Misbegotten</u>, she was the embodiment of lover, mother, and bride, all combined in one magnificent creature. She embraced all those roles, fulfilling them completely, as she did in real life. As for this writer, I shall never forget her performance as Josie. Nor shall I ever forget one precious moment at the Tony Awards ceremony, where I happened to be in her imposing presence. Having accepted her Tony and delivered her acceptance speech--it was late in the evening--she turned straight to the camera; and in that distinctive, throaty voice, said with her feline smile, "OK kids, get to bed!"

NOTES

[1] Michele LaRue, "Dewhurst's Remembrance": Laughing Through Tears," Backstage (September 27, 1991): 3.

[2] LaRue, 3.

[3] Colleen Dewhurst, "The Actress: Colleen Dewhurst: Of My Own Free Will!," The Off-Broadway Experience, Howard Greenberger, ed. (Englewood Cliffs, N.J.: Prentice-Hall, Inc, 1971): 121.

[4] Rex Reed, "But Colleen Almost Does." The New York Times (November 12, 1967): D33.

[5] Charles Moritz, ed. "Dewhurst, Colleen," (New York: The H.W. Wilson Co., 1974): 110.

[6] Judy Stone, "Colleen Dewhurst," Playgirl (April 1975): 89.

[7] Stone, 89.

[8] Moritz, 110.

[9] Stone, 89.

[10] Stone, 89.

[11] Louise Sweeney, "Colleen Dewhurst: America's Mother Courage Now Leaves Them Laughing," The Christian Science Monitor (May 12, 1983): B2

[12] Stone, 89.

[13] T.E. Kalem, "Show Business: Gorgeous Gael," Time (January 21, 1974): 80.

[14] Dewhurst, 113.

[15] Dewhurst, 113.

[16] Dewhurst, 113

[17] Dewhurst, 113.

[18] Dewhurst, 114.

[19] Dewhurst, 115.

[20] Dewhurst, 119.

[21] Sidney Fields, "Only Human: First Twelve Years Are the Hardest!" Daily Mirror (March 4, 1955), n.p. (Clippings, Theatre Collection, New York Public Library).

[22] Dewhurst, 115.

[23] Moritz, 110.

[24] Dewhurst, 122.

[25] Kalem, 80.

[26] Stuart Vaughan, A Possible Theatre (New York: McGraw Hill Book Co., 1965): 40.

[27] Brooks Atkinson. "Shrew in Park: Shakespeare Farce Is Well Produced in the East River Amphitheater." The New York Times(August 26, 1956): II, 1.

[28] Richard Watts Jr., "Two on the Aisle: Random Notes on This and That: Macbeth , " New York Post (August 20, 1957): 32.

[29] Dewhurst, 128.

[30] Dewhurst, 129.

[31] Walter Kerr, "Children of Darkness," New York Herald Tribune (March 1, 1958), n.p. (Clippings, Theatre Collection, New York Public Library).

[32] Richard Watts Jr., "Two on Aisle: M. Camus Studies a Roman Emperor, " New York Post (February 28, 1960). (Clippings, Theatre Collection, New York Public Library).

[33] Richard Watts Jr., "Two on the Aisle: A Striking Drama about Death, " New York Post (December 11, 1960). (Clippings, Theatre Collection, New York Public Library).

[34] Robert Wahls, "Wild Colleen Is Finally Normal, " Daily News (January 1, 1961): 4.

[35] Frances Herridge, "Across the Footlights: Dewhurst Has 'Arrived' on B'way," New York Post (December 23, 1960): 20.

[36] Herridge, 20.

[37] According to Dewhurst in The Off-Broadway Experience, p. 137, George Scott, Quintero, and Theodore Mann as co-producers of the Theatre of Michigan Company had attempted unsuccessfully to set up a

repertoire group in Detroit, Scott's hometown. Two short-lived productions, Ira Levin's General Seeger (2 performances) and Alice Cannon's Great Day in the Morning (10 performances), separately starring Scott and Dewhurst made it to Broadway. To realize his participation, Scott signed a two-year movie contract and sold himself to a television series. Almost at the state of bankruptcy when the project folded, the Scotts moved to Hollywood to work at anything to pay off every cent they owed. Desire Under the Elms brought them back to New York and Off-Broadway.

38 Howard Taubman. "Theatre: St. Louis 1928: Debut for Great Day in the Morning, " The New York Times (March 28, 1962).

39 William Peper, "Colleen Dewhurst Finds Role in Sad Cafe Man-Sized Job," New York World-Telegram and The Sun (October 22, 1963), n.p. (Clippings, Theatre Collection, New York Public Library).

40 Peper.

41 Gene Palatsky. "Star Squares a Wacky Triangle, " Newark Evening News (November 24, 1963): E7.

42 Reed, D33.

43 Reed, D33.

44 Reed, D33.

45 Reed, D1.

46 Michael Iachetta, "The Dark Side of Fair Colleen," Sunday News (December 24, 1972), n.p. (Clippings, Theatre Collection, New York Public Library).

47 Kalem, 80.

48 Howard Kissel, "Colleen Dewhurst (A Moon for the Misbegotten)." Playbill (May 1989): 18.

49 Clive Barnes, "Landmark Moon for the Misbegotten," The New York Times (December 31, 1973): 22.

50 Stone, 89.

51 Stone, 89

52 Stone, 89.

53 Bernard Carrangher, "Personalities: Making It in Showbiz--the Hard Way," Daily News (March 28, 1976). (Clippings, Theatre Collection, New York Public Library).

54 Earl Wilson. "It Happened Last Night: Fraternizing With the Enemy." New York Post (April 6, 1976).

55 Bruce Chadwick, "Colleen Takes Her Act onto the Stage." Daily News (September 26, 1982): 5.

56 Chadwick, 5.

57 John Corry, "A New Test for Colleen Dewhurst," The New York Times (September 26, 1982): C1.

58 Clive Barnes, "You Can't Take It With You: A Family to Adopt." The New York Times (April 5, 1983).

59 Louise Sweeney, "Colleen Dewhurst: America's Mother Courage Now Leaves Them Laughing," The Christian Science Monitor (May 12, 1983): B2.

60 Dewhurst, 135.

61 Moritz, 112.

62 Reed, D33.

63 Colleen Dewhurst," Variety (August 26, 1991): 98.

64 Ann Pinkerton, "Eye View: TV--or not TV?" Women's Wear Daily (August 27, 1976): 44.

65 Maurice Zolotow, "Cleopatra in the Park, " New York Times (June 9, 1968): X3.

66 Robert Windeler, "Colleen Dewhurst Outshines Ingrid Bergman in O'Neill Play," The New York Times (September 14, 1967), n.p. (Clippings, Theatre Collection, New York Public Library).

67 Kay Gardella, "Television: Moon-Struck Colleen Brings Josie to TV," Sunday News (May 18, 1975), n.p. (Clippings, Theatre Collection, New York Public Library).

68 Gardella, n.p.

69 Stone, 48.

70 Michael Buckley, "An Interview with Colleen Dewhurst," TheaterWeek (October 2, 1989: 35.

71 Buckley, 35.

72 Carragher, n.p.

73 Otis Stuart, "Homage: American Classic: Colleen Dewhurst, 1926-1991," Lincoln Center Stagebill (November 11, 1991): 50.

74 Thomas Walsh, "Colleen Dewhurst 1924-1991," Back Stage (August 30, 1991): 5.

75 Walsh, 5.

76 "Colleen Dewhurst Remembered for Roles in O'Neill Plays." The (Torrington, Connecticut) Register Citizen (August 24, 1991): 8.

Productions

The productions listed here are classified according to Stage, Feature Films, Films Made for Television, and Television Episodes, Series, and Specials. They are arranged chronologically by the date of performance. The "See" references indicate related entries in other sections of the book. All abbreviations are explained in the Preface.

STAGE

1946

P1   The Royal Family. Carnegie Lyceum Theatre (Broadway). October 15, 1946. Presented by The American Academy of Dramatic Arts.

Play by George S. Kaufman and Edna Berber

Cast: Colleen Dewhurst (Julia Cavendish), James Vickery (Anthony Cavendish), Rosemary Keck (Della), Robert Anderson (Jo), John Clarke (Hallboy), Joseph Fischer (McDermott), John Wade (Herbert Dean), Dorothy Jackson (Kitty Dean), Elizabeth Carlin (Gwen), Everett Hughes (Perry Stewart), Lucy Lindner (Fanny Cavendish), Samuel Javitz (Oscar Wolfe), Henry Beckman (Gilbert Marshall), William Sater (Gunga), Beth Blossom (Miss Peake)

1952

P2   Desire Under the Elms. ANTA Playhouse (Broadway). Opened January 16, 1952. Closed February 24, 1952, after 48 performances. Presented by Robert Whitehead for the American National Theatre and Academy.

Play by: Eugene O'Neill
Directed by: Harold Clurman
Sets by: Mordecai Gorelik
Costumes by: Ben Edwards

Cast: Dewhurst (A Neighbor), Karl Malden (Ephraim Cabot), Douglass Watson (Eben Cabot), Lou Polan (Simeon Cabot), George Mitchell (Peter Cabot), Carol Stone (Abbie Putnam), Jocelyn Brando (Young Girl), Charles Aidman (Man), Mark Gordon (Fiddler), John McLiam (Another Man), Howard H. Fischer (Old Farmer), Minette Barrett (Woman), Russell Gaige (Sheriff); Elwyn Dearborn, Don Elson, Norma Hayes, George Hoxie, Barbara Schultz, Jutta Wolfe (Neighbors)

Reviews:
Atkinson, Brooks. "At the Theatre." The New York Times
    (January 17, 1952).
Chapman, John. "Desire Under the Elms Remains Powerful, If Just
    a Leetle Quaint." Daily News (January 17, 1952).
Coleman, Robert. "ANTA Puts on Desire Under the Elms." Daily
    Mirror (January 17, 1952).
Hawkins, William. "Desire Under the Elms Revival." New York
    World-Telegram and The Sun (January 17, 1952).
Kerr, Walter. "Desire Under the Elms." New York Herald Tribune
    (January 17, 1952).
McClain, John. "A Powerful Drama, Highly Recommended." New
    York Journal American (January 17, 1952).
Watts, Richard, Jr. "The Tragic Power of Eugene O'Neill." New
    York Post (January 17, 1952).

1954

P3   An Evening With Shakespeare and Marlow. Emmanuel
      Presbyterian Church. Presented by Joseph Papp for the
      Elizabethan Workshop, later called the Shakepearean Workshop,
      which in 1960 officially became the New York Shakepeare Festival.
      Various scenes were presented.

      Dewhurst participated in a reading.

1956

P4   Tamburlaine the Great. Winter Garden (Broadway). Opened
      January 19, 1956. Closed February 2, 1956, after 20 performances.
      Presented by the Producers Theatre (Roger L.
      Stevens, Robert Whitehead, and Robert W.
      Dowling) in association with the Stratford Festival Foundation of Canada.

Play by: Christopher Marlowe
Adapted by: Tyrone Guthrie and Donald Wolfit
Directed by: Guthrie
Sets and Costumes by: Leslie Hurry

Cast: Dewhurst (Turkish Concubine; Virgin of Memphis), David
Gardner (Prologue), Eric House (Mycetes), Tony Van Bridge
(Cosroe), Robert Goodier (Meander), Robert Christie
(Theridamas), Ted Follows (Menaphon), Edward K.
Holmes (Ortygius), Anthony Quayle (Tamburlaine), Barbara Chilcott
(Zenocrate), Donald Davis (Agydas), William Hurt (Techelles),
William Shatner (Usumcasane), Peter Wylde (Scythian Soldier),
Peter Perehinczuk (Persian Spy), Niel Vipond (A Persian
Messenger), Julian Flett (A Scythian Messenger), Deborah Cass
(Anippe), Bruce Swerdfager, (A Basso), Douglas Rain (Bajazeth),
John Hayes (King of Fez), Harry McGirt (King of Morroco), Coral
Browne (Zabina), Margaret Braidwood (Ebea), Lloyd Bochner
(Soldan of Egypt), Roland Bull (King of Arabia), Alan Wilkinson
(Philemus), Louis Negin (Amyras)

Reviews:
Atkinson, Brooks. "Theatre: Tamburlaine the Great a Show-
      Piece." The New York Times (January 20, 1956).
Chapman, John. "Tamburlaine the Great Beats DeMille as a
      Roaring Spectacle." Daily News (January 20, 1956).
Coleman, Robert. "Rip-Roaring Drama at Winter Garden." Daily
      Mirror (January 20, 1956).
Hawkins, William. "Tamburlaine Opens at Winter Garden." New
      York World-Telegram and The Sun (January 20, 1956).
Kerr, Walter. "Theater: Tamburlaine the Great." New York
      Herald Tribune (January 20, 1956).
McClain, John. "Production Is Majestic: Anthony Quayle Heads
      Vast Cast in Violent Elizabethan Drama." New York Journal
      American (January 20, 1956).
Watts, Richard, Jr. "Marlowe's Tamburlaine the Great." New
      York Post (January 20, 1956).

P5   Camille. Cherry Lane Theatre (Off-Broadway). Opened
      September 18, 1956. Closed September 30, 1956. Presented by
      Wayne Richardson.

      Play by: Alexandre Dumas fils
      Produced by: Richardson
      Adapted by: Henriette Metcalf
      Set by: Robert VerBerkmoes
      Costumes by: Adri

      Cast: Dewhurst (Marguerite Gautier), William Major (Baron de
      Varville), Elizabeth Townsend (Nanine), Martha Orrick (Nichette),
      Jo Henderson (Olympe), Donald Marye (Saint Gaudens), Ethel
      Stevens (Prudence), Robert Elston (Armand Duval), Larry
      Swanson (Gaston Rieux), Joseph Barr (M. Duval), Daniel Durning
      (Count de Giray, The Doctor), William Roberts (Gustave), Al Gallo
      (Arthur), Ellena Rafael (Anais)

      Reviews:
      Coleman, Robert. "Theatre: Camille Is Offered at the Cherry
           Lane." Daily Mirror (September 20, 1956).
      Kerr, Walter. "Off-Broadway: Dumas' Camille Revived at Cherry
           Lane Theater." New York Herald Tribune (September 19,
           1956).
      O'Connor, Jim. "Camille: This Revival from French Century Late."
           New York Journal-American (September 19, 1956).
      Watts, Richard, Jr. "Two on the Aisle: The Sad Lady of the
           Camellias." New York Post (September 19, 1956).

      (See also A31, A37.)

P6   The Taming of the Shrew. East River Park Amphitheater. Ran
      July 27-September 7, 1956, on Thursdays and Fridays. Presented
      by Joseph Papp for the Shakespearean Theatre Workshop.

      Play by: Shakespeare
      Directed by: Stuart Vaughan

      Cast: Dewhurst (Katharine), Joseph Barr (Batista), Karl Williams
      (Vincentio), Mel Arrighi (Lucentio), Jack Cannon (Petruchio),
      William Major (Gremio), Robert Baines (Hortensio), Chester
      Doherty (Tranio) John Riordan (Biondello), Hugh Palmerston
      (Grumio), Janis Halliday (Curtis), Larry Swanson (Pedant), Monica

May (Bianca), Rowena Burack (Widow), Daniel Durning (Tailor),
William Roberts (Haberdasher)

Reviews:
Atkinson, Brooks. "Shrew in Park: Shakespeare Farce Is Well
    Produced in the East River Amphitheatre." The New York
    Times(August 26, 1956).
Gelb, Arthur. "The Taming of the Shrew." The New York Times
    (August 11, 1956).

(See also A1, A9.)

P7   Titus Andronicus. Emmanuel Presbyterian Church. Opened
      November 27, 1956. Presented by Joseph Papp for the
      Shakespearean Theatre Workshop.

      Play by: Shakespeare
      Directed by: Frederick Rolf
      Set by: Bernie Joy

      Cast: Dewhurst (Tamora), Leonard Stone (Titus Andronicus),
      Clement Fowler (Marcus Andronicus), James Vickery
      (Saturninus), Roy Bacon (Bassianus), Jack Leckel (Lucius), James
      Glenn (Quintus), David Mauro (Martius), Jim Oyster (Mutius),
      Janice Foley (Young Lucius), Nick Franke (Demetrius), Wayne
      Maxwell (Chiron), Leo Bloom (Alarbus and Clown), Charles
      Meier(Amelius), Alan Howard (Captain,Caius), Peggy Bennion
      (Lavinia), Elizabeth Donnelly (Nurse)

      Review: Gelb, Arthur. "Titus Andronicus." The New York Times
          (December 3, 1956).

P8   The Eagle Has Two Heads. Actor's Playhouse (Off-Broadway).
      Opened December 13, 1956. Closed January 13, 1957, after 38
      performances. A Venture production.

      Play by: Jean Cocteau
      New version by: Stanley Bosworth, Miles Dickson
      Directed by: Dickson

Cast: Dewhurst (The Queen), Iver Fisheman (Felix de Willenstein), Jo Anne Vallier (Edith de Berg), Anthony Vorno (Stanislas), James Earl Jones (Tony), Clement Fowler (Baron de Foehm)

The pseudo-Gothic melodrama tells a tale of a widowed queen, who is isolated in mourning until a poet-assassin creeps through her window and into her heart.

Reviews:
Donnelly, Tom. "Theater: The Queen Was in the Funeral Parlor." New York World-Telegram and The Sun (December 14, 1956).
Gelb, Arthur. "Theatre: Poor Colleen: Miss Dewhurst Dies in Cocteau Revival." The New York Times (December 14, 1956).
Herridge, Frances. "Across the Footlights: Cocteau Play Is a Waste of Talent." New York Post (December 14, 1956).

1957

P9   Maiden Voyage. Forrest Theatre (Philadelphia, Pa). Opened February 28, 1957. Closed March 9, 1957, in pre-Broadway tour. Presented by Kermit Bloomgarden in association with Anna Deer Wiman).

Play by: John Osborn
Directed by: Joseph Anthony
Sets by: Jo Mielziner
Costumes by: Alvin Colt

Cast: Dewhurst (Penelope), Tom Poston (Hermes), Mildred Dunnock (Hera), Melvyn Douglas (Zeus), Valerie Bettis (Calypso), Walter Matthau (Odysseus), Bryarly Lee (Athena), Lee Hays (Telemachus), Bruce Gordon (Antinous), Robert Blackburn (Eurymachus), Carol Gustafson, Shirley Ballard (Handmaidens)

(See A2.)

P10   The Country Wife. Adelphi Theatre. Opened November 27, 1957. Moved to the Henry Miller Theatre December 23, 1957. Closed January 4, 1958, after a total of 45 performances. Presented by the Playwrights' Company, Malcolm Wells, and David Blum.

Play by: William Wycherly
Directed by: George Devine
Sets and Costumes by: Motley

Cast: Dewhurst* (Mrs. Squeamish), Laurence Harvey (Mr. Horner), George Tyne (Quack), Willie Wade (Boy), Ernest Thesiger (Sir Jasper Fidget), Pamela Brown (Lady Fidget), Ludi Claire (Mrs. Dainty Fidget), Richard Easton (Mr. Harcourt), Peter Donat (Mr. Dorilant) John Moffatt (Mr. Sparkish), Paul Whitsun-Jones (Mr. Pinchwife), Julie Harris (Mrs. Margery Pinchwife), Joan Hovis (Lucy), Cynthia Latham (Old Lady Squeamish), David Vaugham (Parson)

*Played Mrs. Dainty Fidget in Washington.

Reviews:
Aston, Frank. "Country Wife Ages Quite Gracefully." New York World-Telegram and The Sun (November 29, 1957).
Atkinson, Brooks. "The Theatre: 200-Year-Old Comedy: The Country Wife Staged at Adelphi." The New York Times (November 28, 1957).
Chapman, John. "The Country Wife a Stylish, Sly Revival of an Old Bedroom Joke." Daily News (November 28, 1957).
Coleman, Robert. "The Country Wife Is Spicy Comedy." Daily Mirror (November 28, 1957).
Kerr, Walter. "First Night Report: The Country Wife." New York Herald Tribune (November 28, 1957).
McClain, John. "Decrepit Romp But Julie Tries." New York Journal American (November 29, 1957).
Watts, Richard, Jr. "Julie Harris Triumphs in The Country Wife." New York Post (November 29, 1957.

P11   Macbeth. Central Park at Belvedere Lake. Opened August 15, 1957. Presented by Joseph Papp for the New York Shakespeare Festival production.

Play by: Shakespeare
Directed by: Stuart Vaughan
Set by: Vaughan, Bernie Joy
Costumes by: Joy

Cast: Dewhurst (Lady Macbeth), George Ebeling (Duncan), Edwin Sherin (Malcolm), Hal England (Donalbain), Roy Poole (Macbeth) Robert Geiringer (Banquo), John McLiam(Macduff), Eb Thomas

(Lennox), Jack Cannon (Ross), Leo Bloom (Angus), Iver Fischman (Caithness), Bill Barcham (Fleance), Richard Durham (Siward), Albert Quinton (Seyton),Gregory Owen (Son to Macduff), Edward Lynch (Doctor), Joseph Shaw (Sergeant), Jerry Stiller (A Porter), Peggy Bennion (Lady Macduff), Zoe Corell (Gentlewoman), Patricia Falkenhain (First Witch) Anne Meara (Second Witch), Patricia O'Grady (Third Witch)

Reviews:
Atkinson, Brooks. "Theater: Macbeth in Park." The New York Times (August 16, 1957).
Beckley, Paul V. "Off Broadway: Macbeth Is Being Staged at Central Park Theater." New York Herald Tribune (August 16, 1957).
Kane, Robert S. "Theater: Park Macbeth Is a Stylish Colorful Drama." World Telegram (August 16, 1957).
Watts, Richard, Jr. "Two on the Aisle: Vigorous Macbeth in Central Park." Daily News (August 16, 1957).

(See also A88.)

1958

P12 Children of Darkness. Circle in the Square, Sheridan Square (Off-Broadway). Opened February 28, 1958. Closed November 16, 1958, after 301 performances. Presented by Leigh Connell, Theodore Mann, and Jose Quintero.

Play by: Edwin Justus Mayer
Directed by: Quintero
Set and Costumes by: David Hays

Cast: Dewhurst (Laetitia), Arthur Malet (Mr. Snap), Rene Zwick (First Bailiff), Ben Hayes (Mr. Cartwright), John Lawrence (Mr. Fierce), Tom Noel (Second Bailiff), Joseph Barr (Jonathan Wild), Jack Cannon (Count La Ruse), George C. Scott (Lord Wainwright)

The tale of Newgate Prison in the days of Jonathan Wild tells of the gang of blackguards, who cozzen and betray one another with good manners and bookish speech.

Reviews:
Atkinson, Brooks. "Theatre: Newgate Prison." The New York Times (March 1, 1958).

Watts, Richard, Jr. "Two on the Aisle: The Skill of Children of Darkness." New York Post (March 16, 1958).

(See also A90, A92, A93.)

P13   A Moon For The Misbegotten. June 5-29, 1958. The Gian-Carlo Menotti Festival of Two Worlds in Spoleto, Italy.

Play by: Eugene O'Neill
Directed by: Jose Quintero

Dewhurst (Josie)

(See A91.)

1959

P14   Antony and Cleopatra. Heckscher Theater (Off-Broadway). Opened January 13, 1959. Closed February 7, 1959, after 23 performances. Presented by Papp for the New York Shakespeare Festival.

Play by: Shakespeare
Directed by: Joseph Papp
Set by: Peter Wexler

Cast: Colleen Dewhurst (Cleopatra), George C. Scott (Antony), David Hooks (Agrippa), Bette Henritze (Charmian), James Frawley (Alexas), Robert Grace (Soothsayer, Menas), John McLiam (Enobarbus), Helena de Crespo (Iras), Edwin Sherin (Octavius Caesar), Thomas Barbour (Lepidus), John Hetherington (Pompey), George Segal (Eros), Anita Stober (Octavia)

Reviews:
Aston, Frank. "Theater: Antony and Cleopatra Opens Run at Hecksher." World Telegram and Sun (January 14, 1959).
Gelb, Arthur. "Antony and Cleopatra Is Presented in Concert Version." The New York Times(January 14, 1959).
Kerr, Walter. "Off-Broadway: Antony and Cleopatra In Revival at Heckscher." New York Herald Tribune (January 14, 1959).
Watt, Douglas. " A Forceful Antony & Cleopatra." Daily News (January 14, 1957).
Watts, Richard, Jr. "Two on the Aisle: A Dynamic Antony and Cleopatra." New York Post (January 14, 1959).
(See also A4.)

1960

P15 <u>Caligula</u>. 54th Street Theatre (Broadway). February 16, 1960.
Closed March 19, 1960. Presented by Chandler Cowles,
Charles Bowden, and Ridgely Bullock.

Play by: Albert Camus
Adapted by: Justian O'Brien
Directed by: Sidney Lumet
Sets and Costumes by: Will Steven Armstrong

Cast: Dewhurst (Caesonia), Frederic Tozere (Octavius), Sorrell
Booke (Darling), Edgar Daniels (Lucius), James O'Rear (Cassius),
Edward Binns (Helicon), Philip Bourneuf (Cherca), Clifford David
(Scipio), Gene Pelligrini (Guard), Kenneth Haigh (Caligula),
Frederic Warriner (Major Domo), Victor Thorley (Mucius),
Harrison Dowd (Mereia), Sandra Kazan (Mucius' Wife), John
Ramondetta (Metulius)

Reviews:
Aston, Frank. "<u>Caligula</u> Scores at 54th." <u>New York World-
Telegram and The Sun</u> (February 17, 1960).
Atkinson, Brooks. "Theatre: <u>Caligula</u> Bows: Camus Drama Opens
at the 54th Street." <u>The New York Times</u> (February 17,
1960).
Chapman, John. "Want to Think? See <u>Caligula</u>." <u>Daily News</u>
(February 17, 1960).
Kerr, Walter. "<u>Caligula</u>." <u>New York Herald Tribune</u> (February 17,
1960).
McClain, John. "Over-Extension of a Small Idea." <u>New York
Journal America</u> (February 17, 1960).
Watts, Richard, Jr. "Two on the Aisle: M. Camus Studies a
Roman Emperor." <u>New York Post</u> (February 17, 1960).

P16 <u>All the Way Home</u>. Belasco Theatre (Broadway). Opened
November 30, 1960. Closed September 16, 1961, after 534
performances. Presented by Fred Coe in association with Arthur
Cantor.

Play by: Tad Mosel
Based on the novel, <u>A Death in the Family</u>, by: James Agee
Directed by: Arthur Penn
Set by: David Hays
Costumes by: Raymond Sovey

Cast: Colleen Dewhurst (Mary Follet), John Megna (Rufus), Arthur
Hill (Jay Follet), Clifton James (Ralph Follet), Lenka Peterson (Sally
Follet), Edwin Wolfe (John Henry Follet), Georgia Simmons (Jessie
Follet), Christopher Month (Jim-Wilson), Dorrit Kelton (Aunt Sadie
Follet), Lyiah Tiffany (Great-Great-Granmaw), Lillian Gish
(Catherine Lynch), Aline MacMahon (Aunt Hannah Lynch),
Thomas Chalmers (Joel Lynch), Tom Wheatley (Andrew Lynch)

This Pulitzer prize winning play is concerned with the effects on a
family of a young father's accidental death, which is seen largely
through the eyes of the small son.

Reviews:
Aston, Frank. "All the Way Home Opens at the Belasco." New
York World-Telegram and The Sun (December 1, 1960).
Chapman, John. "All the Way Home Tender Well Acted, Human,
But Unexciting." Daily News (December 1, 1960).
Coleman, Robert. "All the Way Home Misses Mark." New York
Mirror (December 1, 1960).
Kerr, Walter. "First Night Reports: All the Way Home." New
York Herald Tribune (December 1, 1960).
Taubman, Howard. "Theatre: Version of Agee's Death in the
Family: Miss Dewhurst among Stars at the Belasco." The
New York Times (December 19, 1960).
Watts, Richard, Jr. "Two on the Aisle: A Striking Drama about
Death." New York Post (December 1, 1960).

(See also A94-96.)

1962

P17 Great Day in the Morning. Henry Miller Theatre (Broadway).
Opened March 28, 1962. Closed April 7, after 13 performances.
Theatre of Michigan Company Inc. (Theodore Mann, George C.
Scott).

Play by: O'Neill
Directed by: Jose Quintero
Sets by: Lester Polakov
Costumes by: Noel Taylor

Cast: Dewhurst (Phoebe Flaherty), Peggy Burke (Sis McAnany),
J. D. Cannon (Joe McAnany), Frances Sternhagen (Alice
McAnany), Jeff Herrod (Richie McAnany), Thomas Carlin (Tricky

Hennessey), Eulabelle Moore (Mrs. Grace), Elisabeth Fraser (Dutchy), Gene Roche (Father Finney), Lou Frizzell (Schultz), Clifton James (Brennan Farrell), David Canary (Owen Brady), James Mishler (First Policeman), Michael Bradford (Second Policeman)

Reviews:
Chapman, John. "Great Day in The Morning: Jolly Play for Miss Dewhurst." Daily News (March 29, 1962).
Coleman, Robert. "Great Day Not Great Enough." New York Mirror (March 29, 1962).
Kerr, Walter. "First Night Reports: Great Day in The Morning." New York Herald Tribune (March 29, 1962).
McLain, John. "A Captivating Drama--With Reservations." New York Journal American (March 29, 1962).
Nadel, Norman. "Great Day at Miller's." New York World-Telegram and The Sun (March 29, 1962).
Taubman, Howard. "Theatre: St. Louis 1928." The New York Times (March 29, 1962).
Watts, Richard, Jr. "Two on the Aisle: Joys and Woes of an Irish Family." New York Post (March 29, 1962).

1963

P18   Desire Under the Elms. Circle in the Square (Off-Broadway). January 8, 1963. Closed December 15, 1963, after 384 performances. Presented by Theodore Mann and Jose Quintero.

Play by: O'Neill
Directed by: Jose Quintero
Sets by: David Hays
Costumes by: Noel Taylor

Cast: Dewhurst (Abbie Puttnam), Rip Torn (Eben Cabot), Clifford A. Pellow (Simeon Cabot), Lou Frizzel(Peter Cabot), George C. Scott (Ephraim Cabot), Leonora Landau (A Young Girl), Charles Creasap (A Man), Douglas Roberts (A Fiddler), Jerome Collamore (An Old Farmer), Madeleine Pettet (A Woman), Charles Mundy (The Sheriff); Other Neighbors: Melba De Bayle, Lee Delmer, Sandra Fisher, Sharyn Gans, Carlo Grasso, Marcia Kaufman, Colin Lee, Paul Villani

(See A5, A7, A97, A100.)

P19 Ballad of the Sad Cafe. Martin Beck Theatre (Broadway).
     October 30, 1963. Closed February 15, 1964, after 123
     performances. Presented by Lewis Allen and Ben Edwards.

     Play by: Edward Albee
     Adapted from the novella by: Carson McCullers
     Directed by: Alan Schneider
     Set by: Ben Edwards
     Costumes by: Jane Greenwood

     Cast: Dewhurst (Miss Amelia Evans), Roscoe Lee Browne (The
     Narrator), Louis W. Waldon (Rainey 1), Deane Selmier (Rainey 2),
     John C. Becher (Stumpy MacPhail, William Prince (Henry Macy),
     Michael Dunn (Cousin Lymon), Enid Markey (Emma Hale), Jenny
     Egan(Mrs. Peterson), Roberts Blossom(Merlie Ryan), William
     Duell(Horace Wells), David Clarke (Henry Ford Crimp), Griff
     Evans (Rosser Cline), Nell Harrison (Lucy Willins), Bette Henritze
     (Mrs. Hasty Malone), Lou Antonio(Marvin Macy), Susan Dunfee
     (Henrietta Ford Crimp, Jr.)

     Reviews:
     Bolton, Whitney. "Stage Review: Albee Turns Ballad of the Sad
          Cafe into Intense Experience." The Morning Telegraph
          (November 1, 1963).
     Chapman, John. "Show Business: Albee's Ballad of the Sad Cafe,
          Beautiful, Exciting, Enthralling. " Daily News (November 1,
          1963).
     Kerr, Walter. "Ballad of the Sad Cafe." New York Herald Tribune
          (November 1, 1963),
     McClain, John. "Ballad of the Sad Cafe." New York Journal-
          American (November 1, 1963).
     Nadel, Norman. "Ballad of the Sad Cafe." New York World-
          Telegram and The Sun (November 1, 1963).
     Taubman, Howard. "Theater: The Ballad of the Sad Cafe." The
          New York Times (October 31, 1963).
     Watts, Richard. "Two on the Aisle: Ballad of the Sad Cafe." New
          York Post (November 1, 1963).

     (See also A98, A99, A101, A102, A104.)

P20 Antony and Cleopatra. Delacorte Theater (Off-Broadway). Ran
     June 13-July 6, 1963, for 21 performances. Taped performance
     shown simultaneously over WCBS-TV on June 20. Presented by
     Joseph Papp for the New York Shakespeare Festival.

Play by: Shakespeare
Directed by: Joseph Papp
Set by: Ming Cho Lee
Costumes by: Theoni V. Aldredge

Cast: Dewhurst (Cleopatra), William H. Bassett (Canidius), Stan Dworkin (Taurus), Michael Higgins (Mark Antony), Bette Henritze (Charmian), Frank Shaw Stevens (Alexas), Robert Jackson (Soothsayer), Ramon Bieri (Enobarbus), Ellen Holly (Iras), George Hearn (Scarus), Michael Moriarty (Octavius Caesar), Thomas Barbour (Lepidus), Herb Bernau (First Messenger to Caesar), Joe Allen Dorsey (Second Messenger to Caesar), Clebert Ford (Mardian), Albert Quinton (Maecenas), Mitchell Ryan (Agrippa), Gerald E. McGonagill (Pompey), Anthony Palmer (Menas), Peggy Feury (Octavia), Bill Gunn (Eros), Ray Stubs (Diomedes), Bert Conway (Old Soldier), Maxwell Banks (Egyptian), Leslie Sapiro (Soldier), Ken Hill (First Watchman), Allen Royce (Second Watchman), Charles Durning (Clown)

Review: Funke, Lewis. "Shakespeare Festival Begins in Park." The New York Times (June 21, 1963).

(See also A6, A7, A103, A105.)

1965

P21 A Moon for the Misbegotten. Studio Arena Theatre, Buffalo, NY. Play by: O'Neill
Directed by: Jose Quintero

Cast: Dewhurst (Josie), James Daly (James Tyrone, Jr.), and others.

(See A8.)

1967

P22 More Stately Mansions. Broadhurst Theatre (Broadway). Opened October 31, 1967. Closed March 2, 1968, after 142 performances. Presented by Elliot Martin, in association with the Center Theatre Group, by arrangement with Quinto Productions, production associate Marjorie Martin.

Play: O'Neill
Directed by: Jose Quintero
Set by: Ben Edwards
Costumes by: Jane Greenwood

Cast: Dewhurst (Sara), Barry Macollum (Jamie Cregan), Vincent
Dowling (Mickey Maloy), Helen Craig (Nora Melody), Arthur Hill
(Simon Harford), John Marriott (Cato), Ingrid Bergman (Deborah),
Fred Stewart (Nicholas Gadsby), Lawrence Linville (Joel Harford),
Kermit Murdock (Benjamin Tenard)

Reviews:
Barnes, Clive. "Theater: O'Neill's More Stately Mansions Opens:
      Ingrid Bergman, Miss Dewhurst and Hill Star." The New
      York Times (November 1, 1967).
Chapman, John. "Ingrid Berman Is Back on Stage in Eugene
      O'Neill's Last Big Play." Daily News (November 1, 1967).
Cooke, Richard P. "The Theater: Strained O'Neill." The Wall
      Street Journal (November 2, 1967).
Gottfried, Martin. "Theatre: More Stately Mansions." Women's
      Wear Daily (November 1, 1967).
Kerr, Walter. "No One Will Ever Live in It..." The New York
      Times (November 12, 1967).
Watts, Richard, Jr. "Two on the Aisle: First View of an O'Neill
      Play." New York Post (November 1, 1967).

(See also A107, A108.)

1969

P23 Hello and Goodbye. Sheridan Square Playhouse (Off-Broadway).
     Opened September 18, 1969. Presented by Kermit Bloomgarden in
     association with Commonwealth United Entertainment, and
     Jonathan Burrows.

Play by: Athol Fugard
Directed by: Barney Simon
Set by: William Ritman

Cast: Dewhurst (Hester), Martin Sheen (Johnny)

The play is set in Port Elizabeth, South Africa. A world-wearied
and worn Hester returns to a squalid shack, seeking to claim her
share of an inheritance.

Reviews:

Barnes, Clive. "Theater: A Confrontation: Hello and Goodbye at
    Sheridan Playhouse." The New York Times (September 19,
    1969).
Cooke, Richard P. "The Theater." The Wall Street Journal
    (September 22, 1969).
Newman, Edwin. "Hello and Goodbye." WNBC-TV
    (September 18, 1969).
Silver, Lee. "Colleen and Martin Lift Fugard's Drama." Daily News
    (September 19, 1969).
Watts, Richard, Jr. "Two on the Aisle: Embattled Brother and
    Sister." New York Post (September 19, 1969).
Williams, Christopher. "Hello and Goodbye." Women's Wear
    Daily (September 19, 1969).

1970

P24 The Good Woman of Setzuan. Vivian Beaumont Theatre (Off-
     Broadway. Opened November 5, 1970. Closed December 13, 1970,
     after 46 performances and 13 previews. Presented by the Repertory
     Theater of Lincoln Center (Jules Irving, Robert Symonds).

     Play by: Bertolt Brecht
     Translated by: Ralph Manheim
     Directed by: Robert Symonds
     Sets by: Douglas W. Schmidt
     Costumes by: Carrie Fishbein

     Cast: Dewhurst (Shen Teh), Lou Gilbert (Wang), Philip Bosco
     (First God), Sydney Walker (Second God), Ray Fry (Third God),
     Jack Harrold, Luis Avalos (Gentlemen), Elizabeth Wilson
     (Mrs. Shin), Maury Cooper (Husband), Eda Reiss Merin (Wife),
     Robert Phalen (Nephew), Robert Levine (Unemployed Man),
     Michael Levin (Lin To), Dan Sullivan (Brother), Elizabeth Huddle
     (Sister-in-law), Frances Foster (Mrs. Mi Tzu), Kenneth H. Maxwell
     (Boy), Herbert Foster (Grandfather), Tandy Cronyn (Niece),
     Joseph Mascolo (Policeman), Anne Ives (Carpet Dealer's Wife),
     David Birney (Yang Sun), Florence Tarlow (Old Prostitute),
     Stephen Elliott (Mr. Shu Fu), Priscilla Pointer (Mrs. Yang),
     Luis Avalos (Waiter), Jack Harrold (Priest), James Cook,
     Susan Sharkey (Townspeople), Toby Obayashi, Rebecca Symonds,
     Rico Williams (Children)

Reviews:
Barnes, Clive. "The Theater: Bold Brechtian Parable." The New
    York Times (November 6, 1970).
Chapman, John. "Brecht Drama Assays Business: His & Hers."
    Daily News (November 6, 1970).
Gottfried, Martin. "Theatre: The Good Woman of Setzuan...Uneven
    But Ultimately Satisfying." Women's Wear Daily
    (November 6, 1970).
Kerr, Walter. "Will Brecht Ever Come True?" The New York
    Times (November 15, 1970).
Newman, Edwin. "The Good Woman of Setzuan." WNBC-TV
    (November 5, 1970).
Schubeck, John. "The Good Woman of Setzuan." WABC-TV
    (November 5, 1970).
Watts, Richard, Jr. "Theater: Brecht's Search for Goodness."
    New York Post (November 6, 1970).

1971

P25   All Over. Martin Beck (Broadway). Opened March 27, 1971.
    Closed May 1, 1971, after 40 performances and 14 previews.
    Presented by Richard Barr, Charles Woodward, and Edward Albee.

Play by: Albee
Directed by: John Gielgud
Set and Costumes by: Rouben Ter-Arutunian

Cast: Dewhurst (Mistress), Jessica Tandy (Wife), Madeleine
Sherwood (Daughter), Neil Fitzgerald (Doctor), James Ray (Son),
George Voskovec (Best Friend), Betty Field (Nurse), John Gerstad,
Charles Kindl, Allen Williams (Newspapermen)

Reviews:
Gottfried, Martin. "Theatre: Albee's All Over...Talked to Death."
    Women's Wear Daily (March 29, 1971).
Harris, Leonard. "All Over." WCBS-TV (March 28, 1971).
Kalem, T.E. "Club Bore." Time (April 5, 1971).
Kroll, Jack. "Theater: The Disconnection." Newsweek (April 5,
    1971).
Melloan, George. "The Theater." The Wall Street Journal
    (March 30, 1971).
Newman, Edwin. "All Over." WNBC-TV (March 28, 1971).
Schubeck, John. "All Over." WABC-TV (March 28, 1971).

Watt, Douglas. "Albee's <u>All Over</u> Is Glacial Drama About a Death
  Watch." <u>Daily News</u> (March 29, 1971).
Watts, Richard, Jr. "Theater: The Man Who Lay Dying." <u>New
  York Post</u> (March 29, 1971).

(See also A109, A110.)

1972

P26   <u>Mourning Becomes Electra</u>. Circle in the Square (Joseph E. Levine
      Theatre, Broadway). Opened November 15, 1972. Closed
      December 31, 1972, after 55 performances.

Play by: O'Neill
Director: Theodore Mann
Sets by: Marsha L. Eck
Costumes by: Noel Taylor

Cast: Dewhurst (Christine Mannon), William Hickey (Seth
Beckwith), Hansford Rowe (Amos Ames, Josiah Borden), Eileen
Burns (Louisa Ames, Reverend Everett Hills), Joycelyn Brando
(Minnie, Emma Borden), Pamela Payton-Wright (Lavinia Mannon),
Lisa Richards (Hazel Niles), Jack Ryland (Captain Peter Niles),
Alan Mixon (Captain Adam Brant), Donald Davis (Brigadier
General Ezra Mannon), Daniel Keyes (Dr. Joseph Blake), Stephen
McHattie (Orin Mannon), John Ridge (Chatyman, Ira Mackel),
William Bush (Abner Small)

Reviews:
Gottfried, Martin. "Theatre: <u>Mourning Becomes Electra</u> and a
      Brand New Theatre." <u>Woman's Wear Daily</u> (November 17,
      1962).
Harris, Leonard. "<u>Mourning Becomes Electra</u>." <u>WCBS-TV</u>
      (November 15, 1972).
Kalem, T.E. "The Theater: Day of Wild Wind." <u>Time</u>
      (November 27, 1972).
Kroll, Jack. "Theater: The Circle Moves Uptown." <u>Newsweek</u>
      (November 27, 1962).
Watt, Douglas. "Circle in Square (Uptown) Bows with
      O'Neill Trilogy." <u>Daily News</u> (November 16, 1972).
Watts, Richard, Jr. "Theatre: An O'Neill Masterpiece." <u>New York
      Post</u> (November 16, 1972).
Wilson, Edwin. "The Theatre: A Well-Handled O'Neill Classic."
      <u>The Wall Street Journal</u> (November 21, 1972).

P27 Hamlet. Delacorte Theater (Off-Broadway). Ran June 20-July 16, 1972, for 21 performances. Presented by Joseph Papp for the New York Shakespeare Festival.

Play by: Shakespeare
Directed by: Gerald Freedman
Set by: Ming Cho Lee
Costumes by: Theoni V. Aldredge

Cast: Dewhurst (Gertrude), John Michalski (Bernardo), Roger Brown (Francisco), Robert Stattel (Horatio), Michael Goodwin (Marcellus), James Earl Jones (Claudius), James McGill (Cornelius), Sam Waterston (Laertes), Barnard Hughes (Polonius), Stacy Keach (Hamlet), Kitty Winn (Ophelia), Frank Dwyer (Lucianus), Michael Goodwin (Fortinbras), Greg Wnorowski (Captain), William Robertson (Lord), Nathaniel Robinson, Charles Dinstùhl (Sailors), Anna Brennen (Lady), Charles Durning, Tom Aldredge (Gravediggers), Mel Cobb (Priest), Raul Julia (Osric)

Reviews:
Barnes, Clive. "Hamlet." The New York Times (June 30, 1972).
Gottfried, Martin. "Theater: Hamlet." Women's Wear Daily
    (June 30, 1972).
Kalem, T.E. "The Theater: Willy Loman at Elsinore." Time
    July 10, 1972).
Tallmer, Jerry. "Off-Broadway: I, Claudius." New York Post
    (June 30, 1972).
Watts, Douglas. "Keach Stars in Park." Daily News (June 30,
    1972).
Wilson, Edwin. "The Theater." The Wall Street Journal (July 5,
    1972).

P28 A Moon for the Misbegotten. Morosco Theatre (Broadway).
Opened December 29, 1973. Ran for 175 performances. Presented by Elliot Martin and Lester Osterman Productions (Lester Osterman, Richard Horner).

Play by: O'Neill
Directed by: Jose Quintero
Set by: Ben Edwards
Costumes by: Jane Greenwood

Cast: Dewhurst (Josie Hogan), Jason Robards (James Tyrone Jr.),
Edwin J. McDonough (Mike Hogan), Ed Flanders (Phil Hogan),
John O'Leary (T. Stedman Harder)

Reviews:
Barnes, Clive. "Landmark Moon for the Misbegotten." The New
    York Times (December 31, 1973).
Gottfried, Martin. "Theater: A Moon for the Misbegotten."
    Women's Wear Daily (January 2, 1974).
Harris, Leonard. "A Moon for the Misbegotten." WCBS-TV
    (January 11, 1974).
Holder, Geoffrey. "A Moon for the Misbegotten." WNBC-TV
    (December 29, 1973).
Kalem, T.E. "The Theater: O'Neill Agonistes: A Moon for the
    Misbegotten." Time (January 14, 1974).
Kroll, Jack. "Theater: Battled in Bondage." Newsweek (January
    14, 1974).
Melloan, George. "A Dread Secret Unfolds on a Moonlit Porch."
    The Wall Street Journal (January 2, 1974).
Sanders, Kevin. "A Moon for the Misbegotten." WABC-TV
    (December 29, 1973).
Watt, Douglas. "A Moon for the Misbegotten Back." Daily News
    (December 31, 1973).
Watts, Richard, Jr. "A Play, Superbly Done." New York Post
    (December 31, 1973).

(See also A11, A39, A72, A115-A120.)

1976

P29 Who's Afraid of Virginia Woolf? Music Box Theatre (Broadway).
     Opened April 1, 1976. Closed July 11, 1976, after 117
     performances and 3 previews. Presented by Ken Marsolais and
     James Scott Productions Inc., in association with Richard Barr and
     Clinton Wilder.

     Play by: Albee
     Directed by: Albee
     Set by: William Rittman
     Costumes by: Jane Greewood

     Cast: Dewhurst (Martha), Ben Gazzara (George), Maureen
     Anderman (Honey), Richard Kelton (Nick)

Reviews:
Barnes, Clive. "Stage: Virginia Woolf." The New York Times (April 2, 1976).
Beaufort, John. "Theater: Who's Afraid of Virginia Woolf in Potent Revival." The Christian Science Monitor (April 9, 1976).
Gottfried, Martin. "Woolf Returns with Same Bite." New York Post (April 2, 1976).
Kalem, T.E. "The Theater: Till Death Do Us Part." Time (April 12, 1976).
Kissell, Howard. "Who's Afraid of Virginia Woolf?" Women's Wear Daily (April 2, 1976).
Kroll, Jack. "Theater: Albee's Blackjack." Newsweek (April 12, 1976).
Saunders, Kevin. "Who's Afraid of Viginia Woolf." WABC-TV (April 1, 1976).
Watt, Douglas. "Long Night's Journey Into Day." Daily News (April 2, 1976).
Wilson, Edwin. "Sound and Fury in a Living Room." The Wall Street Journal (April 7, 1976).

(See also A14, A122, A123, A125.)

1977

P30 An Almost Perfect Person. Belasco Theatre (Broadway). Opened October 27, 1977. Closed January 28, 1978, after 108 performances and 5 previews. Presented by Burry Fredrik and Joel Key Rice.

Play by: Judith Ross
Directed by: Zoe Caldwell
Set by: Ben Edward
Costumes by: Jane Greenwood

Cast: Dewhurst (Irene Porter), George Hearn (Dan Michael Connally), Rex Robbins (Jerry Leeds), Gary Alexander Azerier (Announcer's Voice)

A female attorney, who is defeated in a run for Congress, courageously reenters the race, this time for Mayor.

Reviews:
Beaufort, John. "Almost Perfect Person--a Less-than-Perfect Play." The Christian Science Monitor (November 2, 1977).

Eder, Richard. "Drama: Dewhurst Dwarfs Person." The New
  York Times (October 28, 1977).
Gottfried, Martin. "Perfect Person Suffers from Some
  Imperfections." New York Post (October 28, 1977).
Kissel, Howard. "An Almost Perfect Person." Women's Wear
  Daily (October 28, 1977).
Lape, Bob. "An Almost Perfect Person." WABC-TV (October 27,
  1977).
Watts, Douglas. "Comedy with Dewhurst Reopens at Belasco."
  Daily News (October 28, 1977).

(See also A15, A16.)

1978

P31 Are You Now or Have You Ever Been. Promenade Theatre (Off-
     Broadway). Opened October 15, 1978. Moved January 25, 1979 to
     Century Theatre. Closed March 4, 1979, after a total 149
     performances. Presented by Frank Gero and Budd Block. The
     Rutgers Theatre Company production.

     Play by: Eric Bentley
     Directed by: John Bettenbender
     Set by: Joseph F. Miklojcik, Jr.
     Costumes by: Vicki Rita McLaughlin

     Cast: Dewhurst* (Lillian Hellman), Tom Brennan, Robert Nichols,
     Jim Haley (Committee Members), Jerry ver Dorn (The
     Investigator), Gene Terruso, Mary Beth Fisher (The Narrators),
     Jim Haley (Sam G. Wood), Joseph Rose (Edward Dymtryk, Martin
     Berkeley), Benjamin Bettenbender (Ring Lardner, Jr.), Tony
     (Kraber), W. T. Martin (Larry Parks), Frank Gero (Abe Burrows),
     Raymond Baker (Sterling Hayden, Elliott Sullivan), David Francis
     Barker (Elia Kazan, Marc Lawrence), Kevin Motley (Jerome
     Robbins), Tom Brennan (Lionel Stander), Avery Brooks (Paul
     Robeson)

     *Succeeded by: Rosemary Murphy, Frances Sternhagen, Tammy
     Grimes, Barbara Baxley, Peggy Cass, Joan Copeland, Viveca
     Lindfors, Marcella Markham, Liza Minnelli, Louise Lasser, Dina
     Merrill

The action takes place during the hearings before the House Un-American Activities Committee (1947-1956). Dewhurst, as Lillian Hellman, reads a scathing missive to the committee members.

Review: Kerr, Walter. "Are You Now or Have You Ever Been." The New York Times (October 20, 1962).

1979

P32 Taken in Marriage. Public Theater (Off-Broadway).   Ran February 25-March 4, 1979, for 55 performances. Presented by Joseph Papp for the New York Shakespeare Festival.

Play by: Thomas Babe
Directed by: Robert Ackerman
Sets by: Karen Schultz
Costumes by: Bob Wojewodski

Cast: Dewhurst (Ruth Chander), Dixie Carter (Dixie Avalon), Kathleen Quinlan (Annie), Meryl Streep (Andrea), Elizabeth Wilson (Aunt Helen)

Five women are gathered in a New Hampshire church hall for a rehearsal of a wedding that never takes place. The bride's older sister, who is married, has been having an affair of sorts with the bridegroom-to-be.

Reviews:
Barnes, Clive. "Thomas Babe's New Play, a Marriage of Wit and
    Talent." New York Post (February 27, 1979).
Beaufort, John. "Wedding Prelude: Taken in Marriage." The
    Christian Science Monitor (February 28, 1979).
Eder, Richard. "Stage: Thomas Babe's Taken in Marriage at the
    Public Theater." The New York Times (February 27, 1979).
Kalem, T.E. "The Theater: Cornfessional." Time (March 12, 1979).
Kroll, Jack. "Theater: Ladies in Waiting." Newsweek (March 12,
    1979).
Sharp, Christopher. "Theater: Taken in Marriage." Women's Wear
    Daily (February 27, 1979).
Watt, Douglas. "Theater: The Women's Words Just Don't Ring
    True." Daily News (February 27, 1979.)

(See also A20, A21.)

1981

P33 Ned and Jack. Hudson Guild Theatre (Off-Broadway). Opened May 13, 1981. Closed June 14, 1981, after 40 performances. Presented by David Kerry Heefner.

Play by: Sheldon Rosen
Directed by: Dewhurst
Set by: James Leonard Joy
Costumes by: David Murin

Cast: Dwight Schultz (Edward "Ned" Sheldon), Barbara Carusso (Ethel Barrymore), Peter Michael Goetz (John "Jack" Barrymore)

This comedy-drama concerns the fateful encounter between the actor John Barrymore (1882-1942) and his friend the playwright Edward Sheldon (1886-1946). It takes place during the long night following Barrymore's triumphant New York opening of Hamlet in 1922.

Reviews:
Beaufort, John. "Ned and Jack." The Christian Science Monitor (May 26, 1981).
Kerr, Walter. "Ned and Jack." The New York Times (May 31, 1981).
Rich, Frank. "Ned and Jack." The New York Times (May 22, 1981).

(See also P34, A28.)

P34 Ned and Jack. Little Theatre (Broadway). November 8, 1981. Closed after one performance and 10 perviews. Presented by Ken Marsolais and Martin Markinson, All Star Productions Inc., and Axbell Productions Inc.

Play by: Rosen
Directed by: Dewhurst
Set by: Joy
Costumes by: Murin

Cast: John Vickery (Edward "Ned" Sheldon), Sean Griffin (Danny), Barbara Sohmers (Ethel Barrymore), Peter Michael Goetz (John Barrymore), Barton (Charlie)

Reviews:
Beaufort, John. "Ned and Jack." The Christian Science Monitor
(November 12, 1981).
Corry, John. "Ned and Jack." The New York Times
(November 10, 1981).
Rich, Frank. "Ned and Jack." The New York Times (November 9,
1981).

(See also P33, A26, A29, A133, A134.)

1982

P35 The Queen and the Rebels. Plymouth Theatre (Broadway).
September 30, 1982. Closed November 7, 1982, after 45
performances and 19 previews. Presented by special arrangement
with Ken Marsolais and Lita Starr. Circle in the Square production.

Play by: Ugo Betti
Translated by: Henry Reed
Directed by: Waris Hussein
Set by : David Jenkins
Costumes by: Jane Greenwood

Cast: Dewhurst (Argia), Sean Griffin (Porter), Peter Michael Goetz
(Traveller), Donald Gantry (Engineer), Scott Hylands (Raim),
Clarence Felder (General Biante), Anthony DeFonte (Maupa),
Betty Miller (Elizabetta), Christopher Garvin (Boy), Jeffrey Holt
Gardner, Jack R. Marks, Etain O'Malley, Fiddle Viracola, Marek
Johnson, Campbell Scott, Stanley Tucci (Travellers, Soldiers)

The action takes place in a large hall in the main public building of a
hillside village at the present time. Military government officials
attempt to execute their deposed queen.

Reviews:
Beaufort, John. "The Queen and the Rebels." The Christian
Science Monitor (October 12, 1982).
Kerr, Walter. "Stage View: Can't They Do Better by Colleen
Dewhurst?" The New York Times (October 10, 1982),
Rich, Frank. "The Queen and the Rebels." The New York Times
(October 1, 1982).

(See also A30, A32-37, A136, A137.)

1983

P36 <u>You Can't Take It with You</u>. Plymouth Theatre (Broadway).
Opened April 4, 1983. Closed January 1, 1984, after 312
performances. Presented by Ken Marsolais, Karl Allison, Bryan
Bantry; in cooperation with the John F. Kennedy Center for the
Performing Arts.

Play by: Moss Hart and George S. Kaufman
Directed by: Ellis Rabb
Set by: James Tilton
Costumes by: Nancy Potts

Cast: Dewhurst (Olga), Jason Robards (Martin Vanderhof),
Elizabeth Wilson (Penelope Sycamore), Carol Androsky (Essie),
Rosetta LeNoire (Rheba), Jack Dodson (Paul Sycamore), Bill
McCutcheon (Mr. DePinna), Christopher Foster (Ed), Arthur
French (Donald), Maureen Anderman (Alice), Orrin Reiley
(Henderson), Nicholas Surovy (Tony Kirby), James Coco (Boris
Kolenkhov), Alice Drummond (Gay Wellington), Richard Woods
(Mr. Kirby), Meg Mundy (Mrs. Kirby), Page Johnson, Wayne
Elbert, William Castelman (G-Men)

Reviews:
Barnes, Clive. "<u>You Can't Take It with You</u>--Have It." <u>New York
    Post</u> (April 5, 1983).
Beaufort, John. "A Comic Gen Returns to Broadway: <u>You Can't
    Take It with You</u>." <u>The Christian Science Monitor</u> (April 7,
    1983).
Cunningham, Dennis. "<u>You Can't Take It with You</u>." <u>WCBS-TV</u>
    (April 2, 1083).
Kalem, T.E, "The Theater: Loony Bin." <u>Time</u> (April 18, 1983).
Kissel, Howard. "<u>You Can't Take It with You</u>." <u>Women's Wear
    Daily</u> (April 5, 1983).
Kroll, Jack. "The Great Escape As The American Dream."
    <u>Newsweek</u> (April 18, 1983).
Rich, Frank. "Stage: <u>You Can't Take It with You</u>." <u>The New York
    Times</u> (April 5, 1983).
Siegel, Joel. "<u>You Can't Take It with You</u>." <u>WABC-TV</u> (April 2,
    1983).
Watt, Douglas. "A Sweetheart of An Oldie But Goodie Play."
    <u>Daily News</u> (April 5, 1983).

(See also A41, A140, A141.)

1984

P37   Rainsnakes. Long Wharf Theatre (Stage II), New Haven, Conn. Opened November 9, 1984. Presented by special arrangement with Ken Marsolais and I. G. R. Associates, Inc.

Play by: Per Olov Enquist
Translated from Swedish by: Harry G. Carlson
Directed by: Jose Quintero
Set by: John Lee Beatty
Costumes by: James Greenwood

Cast: Dewhurst (Johanne Luise Heiberg), Myra Carter (The Old Bald Woman), William Cain (Johan Ludvig Heiberg), Jeffrey Jones (Hans Christian Andersen)

The play draws on the curious brother-sister relationship between Hans Christian Andersen and the celebrated Danish actress Johanne Luise Heiberg.

(See A43.)

1985

P38   All The Way Home. The National Theatre of the Deaf (Washington, D.C.).

Directed by: Dewhurst.

(See P16, A142.)

P39   A Seagull. Eisenhower Theatre, (Washington, D.C.). December 8, 1985-January 11, 1986. Presented by the John F. Kennedy Center for the Performing Arts (Roger L. Stevens). The American National Theatre production.

Play by: Anton Chekhov
Translated by: Alexander Scriabin
Directed by: Peter Sellars
Sets by: George Tsypin
Costumes by: Kurt Wilhelm

Cast: Dewhurst (Arkadina), Kevin Spacey (Konstantin), Henderson Forsythe (Nickolayevich), Kelly McGillis (Nina), Tony Mockus

(Ilya Shamrayev), Kathleen Nolan (Polina), Priscilla Smith (Marsha), David Strathairn (Boris), Paul Winfield (Dorn), Jan Triska (Semyon), Walter Atamaniuk (Yakou), Marlena Lustik (Cook), Jan Maxwell (Chambermaid), Leslie Amper (Pianist)

Review: Henry, William A. "A Seagull." Time 126 (December 30, 1985).

1987

P40   My Gene. Public Theater (Martinson Hall, Off-Broadway). Ran January 16-March 22, 1987, for 77 performances. Presented by Joseph Papp for the New York Shakespeare Festival.

Play by: Barbara Gelb
Directed by: Andre Ernotte
Costumes by: Muriel Stockdale

Cast: Dewhurst (Carlotta Monterey O'Neill, widow of Eugene O'Neill)

The action takes place in 1968 in a psychiatric ward at St. Lukes' Hospital in New York City. Carlotta O'Neill, the playwright's last wife, reminisces over their turbulent relationship. Mentally unstable, she imagines that she has been committed by her long deceased husband.

Reviews:
Barnes, Clive. "But Where's Gene?" New York Post (January 30, 1987).
Beaufort, John. "Dewhurst on Stage in Work Recalling Life with Eugene O'Neill." The Christian Science Monitor (February 4, 1987).
Cohen, Ron. "My Gene." Women's Wear Daily (January 30, 1987).
Kaplan, Justin. "Stage: Colleen Dewhurst in My Gene." The New York Times (January 30, 1987).
Kissel, Howard. "Long Night's Journey Into Dull." Daily News (January 30, 1987).
Wallach, Allan. "Recalling Life with Eugene O'Neill." New York Newsday (January 30, 1987).
Watt, Douglas. "Second Thoughts on First Nights: The Fault, Dear Reader, Lies Not in the Star." Daily News (February 6, 1987).
(See also A57, A58, A59, A130, A148.)

1988

P41 Ah, Wilderness! Neil Simon Theatre (Broadway). Opened June
     23, 1988. Closed July 19, 1988, after 12 performances and 6
     previews. Presented by Ken Marsolais, Alexander M. Cohen, and
     the John F. Kennedy Center for the Performing Arts, in association
     with the Yale Repertory Theatre.

Play by: O'Neill
Directed by: Jose Quintero
Set by: Michael H. Yeargan
Costumes by: Jane Greenwood

Cast: Dewhurst (Essie Miller), Jason Robards, (Nat Miller), George
Hearn (Sid Davis), Elizabeth Wilson (Lily Miller), Raphael Sbarge
(Richard Miller), Annie Golden (Belle), Kyra Sedgwick (Muriel
McComber), Nicolas Tamarkin (Tommy Miller), Jennnifer Dundas
(Mildred Miller), Campbell Scott (Arthur Miller), William Cain
(David McComber), Jane Macfie (Norah), Steven Skybell (Wint
Selby), Jamey Sheridan (Bartender), William Wise (Salesman)

Reviews:
Barnes, Clive. "O'Neill's Homely Portrait of Family." New York
     Post (June 24, 1988).
Beaufort, John. "Theater: Resonant Comedy Paints Boyhood the
     Way O'Neill Wished It Had Been." The Christian Science
     Monitor (June 27, 1988).
Henry, William A., III. "Ah, Wilderness!." Time (June 27, 1988).
Kissel, Howard. "Tender Trip Back to More Innocent Time."
     Daily News (June 24, 1988).
Rich, Frank. "O'Neill Idealistic Ah, Wilderness!." The New York
     Times (June 24, 1988).
Stearns, David Patrick. "On Stage: O'Neill Centennial Hits a
     Winning Double Play." USA Today (June 24, 1988).
Watt, Douglas. "Second Thoughts on First Nights: Ah,
     Wilderness!." Daily News (July 1, 1988).
Wilson, Edwin. "Ah, Wilderness!." The Wall Street Journal (July
     8, 1988).
Winer, Linda. "The Nice Family that O'Neill Never Had." New
     York Newsday (June 24, 1988).

(See A60, A62, A64, A67, A82, A150.)

P42   Long Day's Journey into Night. Neil Simon Theatre (Broadway).
      Opened June 14, 1988. Closed July 23, 1988, after 28 performances
      and 3 previews. Presented by Ken Marsolais, Alexander M. Cohen,
      and the John F. Kennedy Center for the Performing Arts, in
      association with the Yale Repertory Theater.

      Play by: O'Neill
      Directed by: Jose Quintero
      Set by: Ben Edwards
      Costumes by: Jennifer Tipton

      Cast: Dewhurst (Mary Cavan Tyrone), Jason Robards (James
      Tyrone), Jamey Sheridan (James Tyrone, Jr.), Campbell Scott
      (Edmund Tyrone), Jane Macfie (Cathleen)

      Reviews:
      Barnes, Clive. "Through the Past, Darkly." New York Post
            (June 15, 1988).
      Beaufort, John. "Robard's Long Journey with O'Neill." The
            Christian Science Monitor (June 16, 1988).
      Henry, William A., III. "A Long Day's Journey into Night." Time
            (June 27, 1988).
      Kissel, Howard. "A Worthwhile Journey." Daily News (June 15,
            1988).
      Rich, Frank. "Stars Align for Long Day's Journey." The New York
            Times (June 15, 1988).
      Stearns, David Patrick. "On Stage: O'Neill Centennial Hits a
            Winning Double Play.." USA Today (June 24, 1988).
      Watt, Doug. "Second Thoughts on First Nights: Journey of a
            Lifetime." Daily News (June 24, 1988).
      Wilson, Edwin. "Long Day's Journey into Night." The Wall Street
            Journal (July 8, 1988).
      Winer, Linda. "A Long Day's Journey Revisited." New York
            Newsday (June 15, 1988).

      (See A63-A67, A149-A150.)

                              1989

P43   Love Letters. Edison Theatre (Broadway). October 31-
      November 5, 1989.* Presented by Roger L. Stevens, Thomas
      Viertel, Steven Baruch, and Richard Frankel.

      Play by: A.R. Gurney

Directed by: John Tillinger

Cast: Dewhurst (Melissa Gardner), Jason Robards (Andrew Makepeace Ladd III)

In a wry tale told entirely through letters from their first scrawled valentines of childhood to their last guilty goodbyes, two characters reveal themselves, their love affair, their life-long relationship.

Review: Kerr, Walter. "Love Letters." The New York Times (November 19, 1989).

* The two character stage reading, which was a transfer from the Promenade Theatre (Off-Broadway), featured a a different cast each week.

P44   Elektra. Carnegie Hall. March 3, 1991. The Vienna Philharmonic.

Opera by: Richard Strauss
Libretto by: Hugo Von Hofmannsthal
Adapted from: Sophocles
Directed by: Lorin Maazel

Dewhurst read the libretto in the concert performance of the opera.

Review: Rockwell, John. "Strauss: Elektra." The New York Times (March 4, 1991).

(See also A84.)

FEATURE FILMS

P45 US 1959, The Nun's Story. Warner Brothers.

Produced by: Henry Blanke
Directed by: Fred Zinnemann
Screenplay by: Robert Anderson
Based on the book by: Kathryn C. Hulme

Cast: Dewhurst (Archangel), Audrey Hepburn (Sister Luke, Gabrielle Van Der Mal), Peter Finch (Dr. Fortunati), Edith Evans (Mother Emmanuel, Superior General), Peggy Ashcroft (Mother Mathilde), Dean Jagger (Dr. Van der Mal), Mildred Dunnock (Sister Margharita), Beatrice Straight (Mother Christopher), Patricia Collinge (Sister William)

The film is based on the autobiographical best-seller by Hulme. A Belgian girl (Hepburn) joins a convent as a nursing nun, endures hardship in the Congo, and finally returns to ordinary life. Dewhurst plays a cameo role as a maniacal mental patient.

Review: The New York Times (June 19, 1959).

(See also A75, A92.)

P46 US 1960, Man on a String. Great Britain title, Confessions of a Counterspy. Columbia Pictures.

Produced by: Louis De Rochemont
Directed by: Andre De Toth
Screenplay by: John Kafka and Virginia Shaler
Adapted in part from the book, Ten Years A Counterspy, by: Boris Morros and Charles Samuels

Cast: Dewhurst (Helen Benson), Ernest Borgnine (Boris Mitrov), Kerwin Matthews (Bob Avery), Alexander Scourby (Vadja Kubelov), Glenn Corbett (Frank Sanford), Vladimir Sokoloff (Papa), Frienrich Joloff (Nikolai Chapayev), Richard Kendrick (Inspector Jenkins), Ed Prentiss (Adrian Benson), Roger Ragen (Hans Gruenwald), Robert Iller (Hartman), Reginald Pasch (Otto Bergman), Carl Jaffe (People's Judge), Eva Pflug (Rosnova), Michael Mellinger (Detective)

A Russian-born Hollywood producer, Boris Mitrov, is asked by the Russians to work as a spy in Moscow. He becomes a double agent. Dewhurst plays the wife of an deluded American/Communist party member.

Reviews:
Daily News (May 21, 1960).
New York Post (May 22, 1960).
New York Herald Tribune (May 21, 1960).
The New York Times (May 21, 1960).

P47   US 1966, A Fine Madness. Warner Brothers.

Produced by: Jerome Hellman for Pan Arts
Directed by: Irwin Kershner
Screenplay by: Elliott Baker
Based on his novel of the same name

Cast: Dewhurst (Dr. Kropotkin), Sean Connery (Samson Shillito), Joanne Woodward (Rhoda Shillito), Jean Seberg (Lydia West), Patrick O'Neal (Dr. West), Clive Revill (Dr. Menken), Werner Peters (Dr. Vorbeck), John Fiedler (Daniel Papp), Sue Ann Langdon (Secretary), Kay Medford (Mrs. Fish), Jackie Coogan (Mr. Fitzgerald), Zohra Lampert (Mrs. Tupperman), Bibi Osterwald (Mrs. Fitzgerald), Mabel Albertson (Chairwoman)

In this satire on modern psychiatry, a poet is lobotomized after having an affair with Lydia, the wife of his psychiatrist, and with Dr. Kropotkin (Dewhurst), the psychiatrist's colleague.

Reviews:
The New York Times (June 30, 1966).
Newsweek (June 27, 1966).
Time (July 8, 1966).
Variety (May 4, 1966).

P48   US 1971, The Last Run. Metro Goldwyn Mayer.

Produced by: Carter De Haven
Directed by: Richard Fleischer
Screenplay by: Alan Sharp

Cast: Dewhurst (Monique), George C. Scott (Harry Garmes), Tony Musante (Paul Ricard), Trish Van Devere (Claudie Scherrer), Aldo Sanbrell (Miguel) , Antonio Tarruella (Motorcycle Policeman), Robert Coleby (Hitchhiker), Robert J. Zurica (1st Man), Rocky Taylor (2nd Man)

American mobster, Harry Garmes (George C. Scott), comes out of his retirement of nine years to chase an escaped bandit (Tony Musante) across the Spanish border into France. Van Devere plays the bandit's moll. Dewhurst plays a whore.

Review: Films and Filming (April 1972).

P49   US 1972, Cowboys. Warner Brothers.

Produced, Directed by: Mark Rydell
Screenplay by: Irving Ravetch,
Harriet Frank, Jr., and William Dale Jennings
Based on the novel by: Jennings

Cast: Dewhurst (Madam), John Wayne (Wil Anderson), Roscoe Lee Browne (Cook), Bruce Dern (Rustler), Sarah Cunningham (Saloon keeper), Allyn Ann McLerie (Schoolteacher), A Martinez (Cimarron), Alfred Barker, Jr. (Boy), Nicolas Beauty (Boy), Steve Benedict (Boy), Robert Carradine (Boy), Norman Howell, Jr. (Boy), Stephen Hudis (Boy), Sean Kelly (Boy), Clay O'Brien (Boy)

Wil Anderson leads a group of inexperienced teenagers on a cattle drive and to maturity in this western. Dewhurst plays the madam of a group of traveling prostitutes.

P50   US 1974, McQ. Warner Brothers.

Produced by: Batjac and Levy-Gardner
Directed by: John Sturges
Screenplay by: Lawrence Roman

Cast: Dewhurst (Myra), John Wayne (McQ), Diana Muldaur (Lois), Clu Gulager (Toms), David Huddleston (Pinky), Jim Watkins (J.C.), Al Lettieri (Santiago), Julie Adams (Elaine Forrester), Roger E. Mosely (Rosey), Joe Tornatore (LaSalle), Richard Kelton (Radical), Richard Eastham (Walter Forrester), Dick Friel (Bob Mahoney), Fred Waugh (Bodyguard)

A policeman discovers that his partner was a member of a crooked police ring that stole evidence related to drugs in this contemporary crime action film. Dewhurst plays a bar waitress.

Review: Variety (January 23, 1974).

P51 US 1977, Annie Hall. United Artists.

Produced by: Charles H. Joffe
Directed by: Woody Allen
Screenplay by: Allen and Marshall Brickman

Cast: Dewhurst (Mom Hall), Alvy Singer (Woody Allen), Diane Keaton (Annie Hall), Tony Roberts (Rob [Max]), Paul Simon (Tony Lacey), Carol Kane (Allison), Janet Margolin (Robin), Shelley Duvall (Pam), Christopher Walken (Duane Hall), Donald Symington (Dad Hall), Helen Ludlam (Grammy Hall), Mordecai Lawner (Alvy's Dad), Joan Newman (Alvy's Mom), Jonathan Munk (Alvy at 9), Ruth Volner (Alvy's Aunt), Martin Rosenblatt (Alvy's Uncle), Hy Ansel (Joey Nichols), Rashel Novikoff (Aunt Tessie), Marshall McLuhan (Himself), Dick Cavett (Himself)

Comedian Alvy Singer (Woody Allen), who has broken up with Annie Hall (Diane Keaton), reflects upon himself and the romance. Dewhurst plays Mom Hall.

Reviews:
Newsweek (May 2, 1977).
The New York Times (April 21, 1977).
Time (April 25, 1977).
Variety (March 30, 1977).

P52 US 1978, Ice Castles. Columbia Pictures.

Produced by: Rosilyn Heller and John Kemeny
Directed by: Donald Wyre
Screenplay by: Wyre and Gary L. Bain
Based on a story by: Bain

Cast: Dewhurst (Beulah Smith), Lynn-Holly Johnson (Alexis Winston), Robby Benson (Nick Peterson), Tom Skerritt (Marcus Winston), Jennifer Warren (Deborah Macland) David Huffman (Brian Dockett), Diane Reilly (Sandy)

A promising young figure skater (Johnson) is partially blinded in an accident. She perseveres and becomes a champion. Dewhurst stars as the owner of the rundown Ice Castles skating rink.

(See A17, A19.)

P53   Canada 1978, The Third Walker. Quadrant Films-Wychwood.

Produced by: Melvin Simon
Directed by: Teri McLuhan
Screenplay by: Robert Thom
Based on an original story by: Teri McLuhan

Cast: Dewhurst (Kate MacLean), William Shatner (Munro MacLean), Frank Moore (James MacLean), Monique Mecure (Marie Blanchard), Tony Meyer (Etienne Blanchard), David Meyer (Andrew MacLean), Andree Pelletier (Laura), Simon Rankin (Etienne as a boy), Andrew Rankin (Andrew as a boy), Darren DiFonzo (James as a boy), Diane LeBlanc (Nun), Marshall McLuhan (Voice of the judge)

Male twins, who are mixed up at birth in the hospital and given to the wrong mothers (Dewhurst and Mecure), meet twenty-eight years later at their father's funeral.

P54   US 1979, When a Stranger Calls. Columbia Pictures.
Produced by: Melvin Simon
Directed by: Fred Walton
Screenplay by: Steve Feke and Walton

Cast: Dewhurst (Tracy), Carol Kane (Jill Johnson), Charles Durning (John Clifford), Tony Beckley (Curt Duncan), Rachel Roberts (Doctor Monk), Rutanya Alda (Mrs. Mandrakis), Carmen Argenziano (Doctor Mandrakis), Ron O'Neal (Lieutenant Charlie Garber), Steven Anderson (Stephen Lockart)

This terror-filled story concerns an escaped mental patient who makes menacing telephone calls to a babysitter. Dewhurst plays a barfly who helps the police to trap the caller.

Reviews:
The New York Times (October 12, 1979).
Time (November 12, 1979).

(See also A22.)

P55 Canada, 1979, Arthur Miller On Home Ground.

Produced, Directed by: Harry Rasky
Screenplay by: Rasky

Cast: Dewhurst, Marilyn Monroe, Maureen Stapleton, Clark Gable,
Raf Vallone, Burt Lancaster, Faye Dunaway, Mildred Dunnock, Lee
J. Cobb, Christopher Plummer, Edward G. Robinson, George C.
Scott, Jeni Craden, Harris Yulin, Omi Craden (as themselves)

This documentary, based on film clips, recalls the life and career of
Arthur Miller on the occasion of his sixty-fourth birthday.

P56 Canada 1980, Final Assignment. Inter Ocean Film Sales Ltd.

Produced by: Lawrence Hertzog and Gail Thomson
Directed by: Paul Amond
Screenplay by: Marc Rosen

Cast: Dewhurst (Doctor Valentine Ulanova), Genevieve Bujold
(Nicole Thomson), Michael York (Lyosha Petrov), Alexandra
Stewart (Sam O'Donnell), Richard Gabourie (Bowen)

The film is set in Leningrad, where a reporter uncovers evidence of
unorthodox medical experimentation on Russian children. Dewhurst
plays a Russian scientist.

P57 Canada 1980, Tribute. Twentieth Century-Fox.

Produced by: Joel B. Michaels, Garth B. Drabinsky
Directed by: Bob Clark
Screenplay by: Bernard Slade
Based on the stage-play by: Slade

Cast: Dewhurst (Gladys Petrelli), Jack Lemmon (Scottie
Templeton), Robby Benson (Jud Templeton), Lee Remick (Maggie

Strafton), Kim Cattrall (Sally Haines), John Marley (Lou Daniels), Gale Garnett (Hilary)

A Broadway press agent (Lemmon) learns he has a fatal disease just as his son (Benson) comes to visit. Dewhurst stars as Scottie's acerbic, no-nonsense physician.

Review: Variety (December 3, 1980).

(See also A24.)

P58   US 1983, The Dead Zone. Lorimar/Dino de Laurentiis.

Produced by: Debra Hill
Directed by : David Cronenberg
Screenplay by: Jeffrey Boam
Based on novel by: Stephen King

Cast: Dewhurst (Henrietta Dodd), Christopher Walken (Johnny Smith), Brooke Adams (Sarah Bracknell), Tom Skerrit (Sheriff Bannerman), Herbert Lom (Dr. Sam Welzak), Anthony Zerbe (Roger Stuart), Martin Sheen (Greg Stillson), Nicholas Campbell (Frank Dodd), Sean Sullivan (Herb Smith), Jackie Burroughs (Vera Smith), Geza Kovacs (Sonny Elliman), Simon Craig (Christopher Stuart), Barry Flatman (Walter Bracknell)

Walken stars as a young, shy school teacher who leaves his fiancee, Adams, one night during a rainstorm and gets into a near-fatal accident with a jackknifed trailer truck. When he regains consciousness five years later, he kills a corrupt politician, Sheen, as he "sees" the evil the man will do in the future. The teacher's psychic powers are enlisted by Bannerman to bring justice to elusive killer Dodd, whose mother is played by Dewhurst.

P59   US 1986, The Boy Who Could Fly. Twentieth Century-Fox.

Produced by: Gary Adelson
Directed by: Nick Castle
Screenplay by: Castle

Cast: Dewhurst (Mrs. Sherman), Lucy Deakins (Milly), Jay Underwood (Eric), Bonnie Bedelia (Charlene), Fred Savage (Louis), Fred Gwyne (Uncle Hugo), Louise Fletcher (Psychiatrist)

An autistic child (Underwood), who has not spoken since the death of his parents, is sympathetically encouraged to shed his grief by his girlfriend (Deakins) and schoolteacher (Dewhurst).

Reviews:
The Chicago Sun-Times (September 26, 1986).
The Chicago Tribune (October 1, 1986).

P60 US 1988, Obsessed. Astral Films.

Produced by: Robin Spry, Jamie Brown
Directed by: Spry
Screenplay by: Douglas Bowie

Cast: Dewhurst, Kerrie Keane, Daniel Pilon, Saul Rubinek, Alan Thicke, Lynne Griffin (no character identification available)

Set in Canada, a single mother (Keane) seeks revenge after an American hit-and-run driver (Rubinek) kills her only child.

P61 US 1991, Dying Young. Twentieth Century Fox.

Produced by: Sally Field and Kevin McCormick for Fogwood Films
Directed by: Joel Schumacher
Screenplay by: Richard Friedenberg
Based on the novel by: Marti Leimbach

Cast: Dewhurst (Estelle Whittier), Julia Roberts (Hilary O'Neil), Campbell Scott (Victor Geddes), Vincent D'Onofrio (Gordon), David Selby (Richard Geddes) , Ellen Burstyn (Mrs. O'Neil), Dion Anderson (Cappy), George Martin (Malachi)

A young working-class woman, Hilary O'Neil (Roberts), is hired as a nurse-cook-companion for a wealthy, ill young Victor Geddes (Scott). She helps him during his painful chemotherapy treatments. They fall in love. Dewhurst plays a wise old widow, who reads tea leaves and gives advice.

Reviews:
Entertainment Weekly (July 12, 1991).
The Hollywood Reporter (June 18, 1991).

The New York Times (June 21, 1991).
Newsweek (July 1, 1991).
Rolling Stone (August 8, 1991).
Variety (June 18, 1991).

(See also A83.)

P62   US 1991, Termini Station. Presented by Saturday Plays.

Produced by: Alan King
Directed by: King
Screenplay by: Colleen Murphy

Cast: Dewhurst (Molly Dushane), Megan Follows (Micheline
Dushane), Gordon Clapp (Harvey Dushane), Debra McGrath (Liz
Dushane), Leon Pownall (Charles Marshall), Elliott Smith (Delaney)

This film, which is set in an Ontario mining town, views the world
through the embittered eyes of twenty-year-old Micheline Dushane
and her dotty, alcoholic mother (Dewhurst). Nine years earlier,
Micheline's father took her mother into the woods, aimed a rifle at
her head, and at the last moment turned the gun on himself.

Reviews:
Washington Post (November 1, 1991).
The New York Times (May 31, 1991).
Los Angeles Times (December 13, 1991).

FILMS MADE FOR TELEVISION

1961

P63 No Exit. WNET February 27, 1961. Broadcast as The Play of the
Week episode.

Teleplay by: John Paul Sartre
Translated by: Paul Bowles

Cast: Dewhurst (Inez), Dane Clark (Cradeau), Diana Hyland
(Estelle), Jim Oyster (Bellboy)

Three people, trapped in a room together, settle down to get used to
their surroundings and each other--"the hell" they have made for
themselves.

Reviews:
The New York Times (February 28, 1961).
Variety (March 1, 1967).

1964

P64 In What America. WOR May 1964. Broadcast as a once-a-month
Esso World Theatre special.

Producer: Bert Lawrence
Director: Lawrence

Cast: Dewhurst, George C. Scott, Joanna Miles, Richard Jordan,
Gloria Foster, William Daniels, and others.

The telefilm is an artsy mosaic of American thought, in which Allen
Ginsberg rebukes Walt Whitman's roseate vision, James Agee
confesses suicidal despair, Hedda Hopper perceives the essential
Shirley Temple, and more.

1967

P65 The Crucible CBS May 4, 1967. Broadcast as a special. Presented
by Xerox.

Producer: David Susskind
Director: Alex Segal
Teleplay by: Arthur Miller
Based on the play by: Miller

Cast: Dewhurst (Elizabeth Proctor), George C. Scott (John Proctor), Melvyn Douglas, Tuesday Weld, Fritz Weaver, Henry Jones, Cathleen Nesbitt, Will Geer, Paula Bauersmith, Catherine Burns, Clarice Blackburn, Kathy Cody, Thayer David, Dana Eclar, Louise Stubbs, and others

Review: Variety (May 10, 1967).

1971

P66   The Price. NBC February 3, 1971. Broadcast as an episode of The Hallmark Hall of Fame.

Producer: David Susskind
Director: Fielder Cook
Teleplay by: Arthur Miller
Based on the play by: Miller

Cast: Dewhurst (Esther), George C. Scott (Victor), David Burns (Solomon), Barry Sullivan (Walter)

Review: Variety (February 10, 1971).

1972

P67   The Hands of Cormac Joyce. NBC November 17, 1972. Broadcast as a Hallmark Hall of Fame episode.

Producer: Fred L. Engel
Director: Fielder Cook
Produced by: Fred L. Engel
Teleplay by: S.S. Schweitzer, Leonard Wibberly

Cast: Dewhurst (Mollie Joyce), Stephen Boyd (Cormac Joyce), Dominick Guard (Jackie Joyce), Cyril Cusack (Mr. Reese), Deryck Barnes (Pat Connelley), Lynette Ford (Eilis Connelley), Enid Lorimer (Mrs. Reese), Roz DeWinter (Mrs. Connelley)

A proud fisherman fights to save his land from an approaching storm, as others flee the Irish coast for the mainland.

1974

P68 The Story of Jacob and Joseph. ABC April 7, 1974. A special. Milberg Theatrical Productions; Columbia Pictures Television.

Producer: Mildred Freed Alberg
Director: Michael Cacoyannis
Teleplay by: Ernest Kinoy

Cast: Dewhurst (Rebekah), Keith Mitchell (Jacob), Tony LoBianco (Joseph), Herschel Bernardi (Laban), Harry Andrews (Isaac), Julian Glover (Esau), Yona Elian (Rachel), Yoseph Shiloah (Pharoah), Rachel Shore (Potiphar's Wife), Bennes Maarden (Potiphar), Yehuda Efroni (Reuben), Yossi Graber (Butler), Shmuel Atzmon (Judah), Amnon Meskin (Baker), Zila Karney (Leah), Eli Cohen (Gad), Moti Baharav (Dan), Ilan Dar (Simeon), Menahem Eini (Benjamin), Alan Bates (Narration)

A biblical drama, in two parts--the tale of Jacob and Esau and the legend of Joseph and his brothers.

1975

P69 A Moon for the Misbegotten. ABC May 27, 1975. Broadcast as an ABC Theatre episode. Talent Associates-Norton Simon Inc.

Producer: David Susskind
Directors: Jose Quintero, Gordon Rigsby
Teleplay by: Eugene O'Neill

Cast: Dewhurst (Josie), Jason Robards (James Tyrone Jr.), Ed Flanders, John O'Leary, Edwin J. McDonough

Review: Variety (May 28, 1975).

1979

P70 Silent Victory: The Kitty O'Neil Story. CBS February 24, 1979. The Channing-Debin-Locke Company.

Executive producer: David Devin, Duffy Hambleton
Producer: R. J. Louis
Director: Lou Antonio
Teleplay: Steven Gethers

Cast: Dewhurst (Mrs. O'Neil), Stockard Channing (Kitty O'Neil), James Farentino (Duffy Hambleton), Edward Albert (Tom Buchanan), Brian Dennehy (Mr. O'Neill), Jim Antonio (Charlie), Dr. Sammy Lee (Himself), Richard Balin (Accountant), Hildy Brooks (Interviewer), George Petrie (Warren Porter), Nobel Willingham (First Doctor), Lisa Blake Richards (Orchestra Teacher), Angelique Antonio(Kitty-age 2-4), Elkin Antonio (Kitty, age 8-10), Andrius Babusis (Child), George Boyd (Second Teacher), Joan Corley (Child), Norman Field (First Director), Mel Gallagher (Second Doctor), Adam Kaish (Child), Ken Kane (Third Director), Janice Karman (Third Teacher), Fred Lerner (Second Man), Jack Lucarelli (Salesman), Jim Normandin (Third Doctor), Juliet Qualls (Child), Sybil Sondergaard (Crewman), Franko C. Spolar (Assistant Director), Gene Tyburn (CB Man), Robby Weaver (Second Director), William Wheatley (Desk Clerk), George Wilbur (Bank Clerk), Janet Winter (Receptionist)

This telefilm is the real-life story of a deaf girl who becomes one of Hollywood's top stunt-women and holder of the women's land-speed record in a rocket-powered racing car. Dewhurst was nominated for an Emmy Award as Outstanding Supporting Actress.

P71   Studs Lonigan (miniseries). NBC. March 7, 14, 21, 1979.

Executive producer: Lee Rich, Philip Capice
Producer: Harry R. Sherman
Director: James Goldstone
Teleplay by: Reginald Rose
From the book by: James T. Farrell

Cast: Dewhurst (Mary Lonigan), Bill "Studs" Lonigan (Harry Hamlin), Brad Dourif (Danny O'Neill), Charles Durning (Paddy Lonigan), Lisa Pelikan (Lucy Scablon), Diana Scarwid (Catherine Banahan), John Friedrich (Martin Lonigan), James Callahan (Moxey), Devon Ericson (Loretta Lonigan), Sam Weisman (Davey Cohen), David Wilson (Weary Riley), Jed Cooper (Phil Rolfe), Dan Shor (Young Studs), Kevin O'Brien (Young Danny), Corey Pepper (Young Weary), Keith Gordon (Young Paulie), Glenn Withrow (Young Red Kelly), Michael K. Haggerty (Paulie

Haggerty), Dolph Sweet (Father Gilhooley), Laurie Heineman (Eileen Haggerty), Leslie Ackerman (Helen Borax), Richard B. Shull (Davey's Father), Nora Heflin (Sally-Prostitute), Anne Seymour (Nurse), and others.

This six-hour television adaptation of the Farrell trilogy ("Young Lonigan," "The Young Manhood of Studs Lonigan," and "Judgment Day") centers on the struggles and growing pains of a self-destructive Depression-era Chicago youth.

Review: The New York Times (March 7, 1979).

P72　And Baby Makes Six. NBC October 22, 1979. Alan Landsburg Productions.

Executive producer: Alan Landsburg, Sonny Fox
Supervising producer: Herbert Hirschman
Producer: Kay Hoffman, Shelley List
Director: Waris Hussein
Teleplay by: List

Cast: Dewhurst (Anna Kramer), Warren Oates (Michael Kramer), Maggie Cooper (Elizabeth Winston), Al Corley (Franklyn Kramer), Timothy Hutton (Jason Kramer), Allyn Ann McLerie (Dora), Mildred Dunnock (Serena Fox), Mason Adams (Dr. Eliot Losen), Maria Melendez (Marta Montez), Bill Smillie (Pharmacist), Lee Wallace (Sam Blumenkrantz), Christopher Allport (Jeff Winston), Tamu (Donna, Housekeeper), Joshua Grenrock (Alex), Richard Roat (Bill Finley), Rita Silvera (Nurse)

A middle-aged couple (Dewhurst and Oates) with three grown children discover they will soon be parents. A sequel, Baby Comes Home, follows in 1980.

Review: The New York Times (October 22, 1979).

(See also P79.)

P73　Mary and Joseph: A Story of Faith. NBC December 9, 1979. Astral Films; Lorimar Productions.

Executive producer: Lee Rich, Harold Greenberg
Producer: Gene Corman

Director: Eric Till
Teleplay by: Carmen Culver

Cast: Dewhurst (Elizabeth), Blanche Baker (Mary), Lloyd Bochner (Matthew), Shay Duffin (Bartholomew), Jeff East (Joseph), Paul Hecht (Joachim), Marilyn Lightstone (Anna), Murray Matheson (Zacharias), Stephen McHattie (Judah), Tuvia Tavi (Demetrius), Dina Dovon (Esther), Gabi Amrani (Shem), Joseph Bee (Young Zealot), Jacob Ben Shira (Shopkeeper); With: Yossi Yadin, Amos Mokadi, Noam Kedem, Liron Nirgad, Yehuda Efroni, Yakar Semach, Israel Biderman

This telefilm is based on the birth of Christ and its effects upon the lives of well-known Biblical figures of the time.

1980

P74   Death Penalty. NBC January 22, 1980. Brockway Productions; NBC Entertainment.

Executive producer: Herbert Brodkin
Producer: Robert 'Buzz' Berger
Director: Waris Hussein
Teleplay by: Edward Adler

Cast: Dewhurst (Elaine Lipton), Dana Elcar (John Mulligan), Joe Morton (William Terry), David Labiosa (Carlos Rivera) Ted Ross (Woody), Dan Hedaya (Detective Ralph Corso), Marcelino Sanchez (Paco Sanchez), Sarah Natoli (Francine Rosario), Paul McCrane (Joey Rodick), James Baffico (Captain Leibowitz), Alba Oms (Maria Lopez), Frank Robles (Luiz Lopez), Thomas Hill (Trial Judge), David Harris (Claudell), E. Brian Dean (Keller), Clayton Hill (Bailiff), Hugh Rose (Jury Foreman), Marty Chill (Cop)

Strong-willed psychologist Dr. Lipton (Dewhurst) attempts to rehabilitate a gang member, who has killed two teenagers in a rumble.

Review: The New York Times (January 22, 1980).

(See also A23, A128.)

P75   Escape. CBS February 20, 1980. Henry Jaffee Enterprises.

Executive producer: Henry Jaffee, William Beaudine, Jr.
Producer: Michael Jaffee
Director: Robert Michael Lewis
Teleplay by: Michael Zagor
From the book by: Dwight Worker, Barbara Worker

Cast: Dewhurst (Lily Levison), Timothy Bottoms (Dwight Worker), Kay Lenz (Barbara Chilcoate), Miguel Angel Suarez (Fernando Gardner-Pasquel), Sandra Alexander (Gabrielle), Allan Miller (Jack Branch), Antonio Fargas (Jaime Valdez), Vincent Schiavelli (J. W. White), Jorge Cervera (Tierno), Elliott Street (Roger Brody), Louis Giambalvo (Hank), Philip Levien (Steven), William Marquez (Colonel Fuentes), Tina Menard (Lupe), Ernie Fuentes (Guard), Rick Garcia (1st Commando), Bert Santo (2nd Commando), Larry Duran (Arturo), Tiger Perez (Alfredo), Luis Lopez Casanova (Little Guard)

This telefilm is based on the true story of Dwight Worker, an American jailed in Mexico for drug charges. His escape is the only one from Lecumberri Prison since Pancho Villa.

P76   Guyana Tragedy: The Story of Jim Jones. CBS April 15-16, 1980.
The Konigsberg Company (120 mins each part; 4 hrs total)

Executive producer: Frank Konigsberg
Producer: Ernest Tidyman, Sam Manners
Director: William A. Graham
Teleplay: Tidyman
From the book Guyana Massacre: The Eyewitness
   Account by: Charles A. Krause and The Washington Post Staff

Cast: Dewhurst (Myrtle Kennedy), Powers Boothe (Reverend Jim Jones), Ned Beatty (Congressman Leo J. Ryan), Irene Cara (Alice Jefferson), Veronica Cartwright (Merceline Jones), Rosalind Cash (Jennie Hammond), Brad Dourif (David Langtree), Meg Foster (Jean Ritchie), Michael C. Gwynne (Larry King), Albert Hall (Otis Jefferson), Linda Haynes (Karen Bundy), Diane Ladd (Lynetta Jones), Ron O'Neal (Colonees Robles), Randy Quaid (Clayton Ritchie), Diana Scarwid (Sheila Langtree), Madge Sinclair (Mrs. Jefferson), Brenda Vaccaro (Jane Briggs), LeVar Burton (Richard Jefferson), Clifton James (Barber Charlie Amos), Ed Lauter (Jim Jones, Sr.), James Earl Jones (Father Divine), Dimitra Arliss (Sister Fleming), David Hubbard (Raymond Jefferson), John Dukakis (Jack Daniels), Benji Wilhoite (Jim Jones, as Boy), Ralph Pace(Mr.

Hester), William Dozier (Mr. Caldwell), Paul Wallace (Charlie Fishback), Walter M. Elder, Sr. (Mr. Holloway), Martha Knighton (Mrs. Kruger), Guy Del Russo (1st Reporter), Richard Reiner (2nd Reporter), Tony Foster (Joshua), Danny Nelson (Mr. Stevens), Georgia Allen (Sister Carmella), Mildred Brown (Sister Crandall), Roy Tatum (Brother Morris), Bernardine Mitchell (Black Woman), Charlie Anderson (Hoodlum), Alvin Pealer (George), Charlie Franzen (Phil), Les Hatfield (Klan Leader), Buzzy Hill (Albert), Joe Dorsey (Jakes), Henry Lide (Mr. Brooks), Terry Browning (Cashier), Bernice Ramsey (Angel), Frank Konigsberg (3rd Reporter), Savino Maneri (Defector), Tony King (Choate), Joel Godard (John Briggs), Meg Brush (Mrs. Briggs), Dolores Robinson (New Arrival), Vivian Edwards (Mrs. Halperin), Luther McLaughlin (Elderly Man), Steve Grand (Temple Member), Peter Moldonado (Guard), Pedro Ilerio (Black Temple Member), Bill Coyne (White Temple Member), Annie Feliciana (Woman), Rita Byrd (Mrs. Manners)

This two-part, four-hour film is based on the true story of Reverend Jim Jones, the self-styled preacher who led the settlers of Jonestown, Guyana, to mass suicide in late 1978. It received an Emmy nomination as Outstanding Drama Special.

P77   The Women's Room (series). ABC September 14, 1980. Philip Mandelker Production; Warner Brothers Television.

Executive producer: Philip Mandelker
Producer: Kip Gowans, Anna Cottle
Director: Glenn Jordon
Teleplay: Carol Sobieski
From the novel by: Marilyn French

Cast: Dewhurst (Val), Lee Remick (Mira Adams), Patty Duke Astin (Lily), Kathryn Harrold (Bliss), Tovah Feldshuh (Iso), Tyne Daly (Adele), Lisa Pelikan (Kyla), Heidi Vaughn (Samantha), Mare Winningham (Chris), Ted Danson (Norm), Gregory Harrison (Ben Volper), Jenny O'Hara (Mrs. Martinelli), Christopher Pennock (Harley), Al Corley (Tad Ford), Michael LeClair (Normie, age 15), Johnny Timko (Clark, age 14), Drew Snyder (Carl); With: Richard Coyle, Steven Gagnon, Naomi White, Patricia Wilson, Lew Horn, Karen Howard, Enid Kent, Douglas Stevenson

In this sudsy adaptation of Marilyn French's feminist novel, which spans the 1950s and 1960s, a troubled divorcee (Remick) ultimately becomes a professor to the cheers of her sister suburban matrons. Dewhurst was nominated for an Emmy as Outstanding Supporting Actress. An Emmy nomination went to the film as Outstanding Drama Special.

P78   A Perfect Match. CBS October 5, 1980. Lorimar Productions.

Executive producer: Lee Rich, David Jacobs
Producer: Andre Guttfreund
Director: Mel Damski
Teleplay: John Sayles
From the story by: Guttfreund, Mell Damski

Cast: Dewhurst (Meg Larson), Linda Kelsey (Miranda McLloyd), Michael Brandon (Steve Triandos), Lisa Lucas (Julie Larson), Charles Durning (Bill Larson), Clyde Kusatsu (Dr. Tommy Chang), Bonnie Bartlett (Judge Greenberg), Hildy Brooks (Esther), Alexa Kenin (Angel), Bever-Leigh Banfield (Rhonda), Marilyn Kagan (Lisa), Darian Mathias (Ann), Alvin Hammer (Leo), Peter Lempert (Specs), Michael Currie (Dr. Banks), John Clavin (Stewart), Daniel Nunez (Boy), Susie Coelho (Margo), Christine Dickinson (Lexie), Zoey Wilson (Helen), Gayanne Meyers (Tara), Lani McKee (Nurse)

A successful fashion designer, Miranda McLloyd, who has a threatening disease, searches and finds the one suitable donor for a bone marrow transplant--the daughter she gave up for adoption years ago. Dewhurst and Durning play the adoptive parents.

Review: The New York Times (October 3, 1980).

P79   Baby Come Home. CBS October 16, 1980. Alan Landsburg Productions.

Executive producer: Alan Landsburg
Producer: Shelley List, Kay Hoffman
Director: Waris Hussein
Teleplay: List

Cast: Dewhurst (Anna Kramer), Warren Oates (Michael Kramer), Devon Ericson (Elizabeth Winston), Fredric Lehne (Franklin Kramer), Christopher Marcantel (Jason Kramer), Mildred Dunnock (Serena), Paul McCrane (Bobby Moore), David Huffman (Jeff

Winston), Dena Dietrich (Dora), James Nobel (Dr. Elliott Losen), Lee Wallace (Sam Blumenkrantz), Floyd Levine (Louis Zambello), Toni Gellman (Loretta Zambello), Maria Melendez (Marta Kramer), Mel Stewart (Mr. Adams), John Medici (Officer Caputo), Janice Kent (Attractive Girl in Car), Archie Lang (Delivery Room Doctor), George Caroll (Umberto)

In this sequel to And Baby Makes Six (1979), the middle-aged couple with grown children (Dewhurst and Oates) restructure their lives with the advent of their new baby.

(See P72.)

1981

P80   A Few Days in Weasel Creek. CBS October 21, 1981. Hummingbird Productions Inc. Warner Brothers Television.

Executive producer: Cyma Rubin
Producer: Robert L. Jacks
Director: Dick Lowry
Teleplay by: Durrell Royce Crays
From the book by: Joanna Brent

Cast: Dewhurst (Cora Jackfield), Mare Winningham (Locksley Claitor), John Hammond (Beldon Stokes), Kevin Geer (Calvin Stokes), Nicholas Pryor (Edwin Potter), Glen Morshower (Eugene), Tracey Gold (Buddy), Richard Farnsworth (Jason Stayvey), Barry Corbin (Gus Lobell), Robert Carnegie (Bob Riggins), Michael Keenan (Sarpey), Amzie Strickland (Maribeth Stayvey), John Bellah (Nolan), Kim Bronson (Jolene), Johnnie Collins III (Station Attendant), Ernest Harada (Papa Tourist), Karyn Harrison (La Verne), Sally Imamura (Baby Tourist), Kathy Kartiganer (Calvin's Wife), Randy Patrick (Dewey), Elsa Raven (Station Owner), Lucy Webb (Darlene), Carol Ann Williams (Bebe), Trey Wilson (Lester), Momo Yashima (Mama Tourist)

This serio-comic road telefilm tells the story of a feisty girl (Winningham), who sets out for California and hitches a ride for herself and her house trailer with a runaway farm boy (Hammond) and his pickup truck. The two stop in Weasel Creek to deliver a tablecloth to his Aunt Cora (Dewhurst).

Review: The New York Times (October 21, 1981).

1982

P81   The Blue and the Gray (miniseries). CBS November 14, 16, 17,
      1982. White/Reda Productions; Columbia Pictures Television (180
      mins. parts one and three; 120 mins. part two; 8 hrs total)

Executive producer: Larry White, Lou Reda
Producer: Hugn Benson, Harry Thomason
Director: Andrew V. McLaglen
Teleplay: Ian McLellan Hunter
From a story by: Bruce Catton, John Leekley

Cast: Dewhurst (Maggie Geyser), Stacy Keach (Jonas Steele), John
Hammond (John Geyser), Diane Baker (Evelyn Hale), Kathleen
Beller (Kathy Reynolds), Paul Benedict (Arbuthnot), Lloyd Bridges
(Ben Geyser), Rory Calhoun (General George Meade), David Doyle
(Phineas Wade), Michael Horton (Mark Geyser), Warren Oates
(Preacher,Major Welles), Gerald S. O'Loughlin (Sergeant O'Toole),
Geraldine Page (Mrs. Lovelace), Dan Shor (Luke Geyser), Rip
Torn (Gen. Ulysses S. Grant), Robert Vaughn (Senator Reynolds),
John Vernon (Secretary of State Seward), Sterling Hayden (John
Brown), Paul Winfield (Jonathan Henry), Gregory Peck (Abraham
Lincoln), Julia Duffy (Mary Hale), Robin Gammell (Jacob Hale, Sr.),
David W. Harper (James Hale), Julius Harris (Swampt Preacher),
Gregg Henry (Lester Bedell), Cooper Huckabee (Matthew Geyser),
James Carroll Jordan (Professor Lowe), Brian Kerwin (Malachy
Hale), Bill Lucking (Captain Potts), Charles Napier (Major
Harrison), Walter Olkewicz (Private Grundy), Penny Peyser (Emma
Geyser), Duncan Regehr (Captain Randolph), David Rounds
(Christopher Spencer), Christopher Stone (Major Fairbairn), Bruce
Abbott (Jake Hale, Jr.), Royce D. Applegate (1st Cell Reporter),
Walter Brooke (Gen. Herman Haupt), Janice Carroll (Mary Todd
Lincoln), Fredric Cook (Captain Grimes), William Brian Curran
(Dr. Bennett), Alex Harvey (Calvary Colonel), John Dennis Johnston
(Lieutenant Hardy), Steve Nevil (Johnny Reb), Gregg Palmer (Bull
Run Colonel), George Petrie(Court Clerk), Veronica Redd (Hattie),
Jordan Rhodes (Pennsylvania Colonel), Warwick Sims (Count Von
Ziller), Fred Stuthman (George), Robert Symonds (General Robert
E. Lee), Matthew Tobin (James Hale's Doctor), Peter Von Zerneck
(Prussian General), Len Wayland (Balloon Field General), Maggie
Wellman (Nell), William Wellman, Jr. (Lieutenant Mercer), Noble
Willingham (Field)

This sweeping Civil War saga took eight hours to unfold over three
nights. It was adapted from historian Bruce Catton's book and

garnered four Emmy nominations for photography (part 3), music (part 2), editing (part 1), and sound editing (part 1).

Review: The New York Times (November 14, 1982).

1984

P82 The Glitter Dome. HBO November 18, 1984. Telepictures Corporation; Trincomali Film Productions; HBO Premier Films.

Executive producer: Frank Konigsberg
Producer: Stuart Margolin, Justis Greene
Director: Margolin
Teleplay: Stanley Kallis
From the novel by: Joseph Wambaugh

Cast: Dewhurst (Lorna Dilman), James Garner (Al Mackey), Margot Kidder (Willie), John Lithgow (Marty Welborn), John Marley (Captain Woofer), Stuart Margolin (Herman Sinclair), Paul Koslo (Griswold Veals), Alex Diakun (Weasel), Billy Kerr (Ferret), William Taylor (Officer Gibson Hand), Dusty Morean (Buckmore Phipps), Christianne Hirt (Peggy Farrell/ 'Jill', Tom McBeath (Flameout Farrell), Dixie Seatle (Amazing Grace), Dale Wilson (Lloyd Bozeman), Julian Munoz (Elliot Ramos), Sal Lopez (Chucy), Real Andrews (Maxine), Stephen Chang (Minh Nguyen), Dawn Luker (Gladys), Claudine Melgrave (Yacht Woman), Colin Skinner (Yacht Man), Harvey Miller (Harvey Himmelfarb), Enid Saunders (Eleanor St. Denis), Alistair MacDuff (Malcolm Sinclair), Clara Kamuude (Whore), William Nunn (Detective Simon), Preston Ford (Detective Shultz), Beau Kazar (Hockey Player), Christopher Martini (Danny), Michelle Martini (Karen), Max Martini (Steven), Benson Fong (Wing, the Bartender)

In this adaptation of the Wambaugh novel, two L.A. detectives (Garner and Lithgow) look for the murderer of a film mogul and get involved with Hollywood's drug dealers, hustlers, kinky actresses, and sadistic killers. Dewhurst plays a tough and menacing lesbian.

Review: Variety (November 28, 1984).

1985

P83 A.D. (miniseries). NBC March 31-April 4, 1985. Procter & Gamble
Productions; International Film Productions (180 mins. each parts
one and five; 120 mins. each part two through four, 12 hrs.
total)

Supervising producer: John A. Martinelli
Producer: Vincenzo Labella
Director: Stuart Cooper
Teleplay: Labella

Cast: Dewhurst (Antonia), Anthony Andrews (Nero), Ava
Gardner (Agrippina), David Hedison (Porcius Festus), John
Houseman (Gamaliel), Richard Kiley (Claudius), James Mason
(Tiberius), John McEnery (Caligula), Ian McShane (Sejanus),
Jennifer O'Neill (Messalina), Millie Perkins (Mary), Denis Quilley
(Peter), Fernando Rey (Seneca), Richard Roundtree (Serpenius),
Susan Sarandon (Livilla), Ben Vereen (Ethiopian), Tony Vogel
(Aquila), Jack Warden (Nera), Anthony Zerbe (Pontius Pilate), Neil
Dickson (Valerius), Cecil Humphreys (Caleb), Amanda Pays
(Sarah), Philip Sayer (Paul/Saul), Diane Venora (Corinna), Michael
Wilding (Jesus), Vincenzo Ricotta (Stephen), Rebecca Saire (Ruth),
Tom Durham (Cleopas), Anthony Pedley (Zachaeus), Harold
Kasket (Caiaphas), Ralph Arliss (Samuel), Mike Gwilym (Pallas),
David Harris (Thomas), Norma Martinelli (Apicata), Bruce
Winant (Seth), Jonathan Hyde (Tigellinus), Damien Thomas (Herod
Agrippa), Derek Hoxby (Agrippa II), Angela Morant (Priscilla),
Clive Arrindell (Cassius Chaerca), Paul Freeman (Cornelius),
Andrea Prodan (Brittanicus), Akosua Busia (Acte), Vernon
Dobtcheff (Flavius Sabinus), Gerrard McArthur (Luke), Jane
Howe(Poppea), Jonathan Tafler (Aaron), Richard Kane (Agrippa
III), Barrie Houghton (Ananias the Essene), Maggie Wickman
(Apicata), Alan Downer (Barnabas), Martin Potter (Gaius
Calpernius Piso), Colin Haigh (James), Philip Anthony (James, the
Elder), Renato Scarpa (Lucius Marinus), Roderick Horn
(Marcellus), John Wheatley (Marcus I), Joss Buckley (Matthew),
David Sumner (Mathias), Stephen Finlay (Nicanor), Katia
Thandoulaki (Octavia), Eddie Grossman (Parmenas), David
Haughton (Petronius), John Steiner (Simon the Magus), Robert
Wentz (Thrasyllus)

This twelve hour mini-series is a lavish $30-million epic filmed in
Tunisia with 400 speaking parts and a cast of thousands. A successor
of sorts to Jesus of Nazareth, it covers the years 30-69 A.D. and the

rising conflict between the Jewish zealots, the early Christians, and the Roman Empire.

1986

P84   Anne of Green Gables (series). PBS February 16, 1986 to March 9, 1986. Kevin Sullivan Films, Canada.

Executive producer: Sullivan, Ian McDougall
Director: Sullivan
Teleplay by: Sullivan, Joe Wiesenfeld
Based on the novel by: Lucy Maud Montgomery

Cast: Dewhurst (Marilla Cuthbert), Anne Shirley (Megan Follows), Richard Farnsworth (Matthew Cuthbert), Schuyler Grant (Diana Barry), Jonathan Crombie (Gilbert Blythe), Patricia Hamilton (Rachel Lynde)

Spinster Marilla Cuthbert and her bachelor brother send for an orphan boy to help them at their home, Green Gables, on Canada's Prince Edward Island. By mistake, Anne Shirley is sent instead. Her "queer ways" endear her to the Cuthberts.

Reviews:
The New York Times (February 14, 1986).
Variety (December 11, 1985).

(See also A47, A74, A146.)

P85   Between Two Women. ABC March 10, 1986. Jon Avnet Company.

Executive producer: Jon Avnet
Producer: Carol Schreder
Co-producer: Polly Platt
Director: Avnet
Teleplay: Larry Grusin, Avnet
From the novel, Living Arrows, by: Gillian Martin

Cast: Dewhurst (Barbara Petherton), Farrah Fawcett (Val Petherton), Michael Nouri (Harry Petherton), Bridgette Andersen (Kate Petherton), Danny Corkill (Sandy Petherton), Steven Hill (Teddy Petherton), Terry O'Quinn (Dr. Wallace), Kenneth Danziger

(Charles), Carmen Argenziano (Robert Walker), Bronson Pinchot (Photographer)

This telefilm adaptation of the Gillian Martin novel brings together an overbearing, ex-opera diva mother (Dewhurst) and her school teacher daughter-in-law (Fawcett) in a dramatic clash of wills that ends when the older woman has a stroke. Dewhurst won an Emmy as Outstanding Supporting Actress.

Review: Variety (March 26, 1986).

P86   Johnny Bull. ABC May 19, 1986. Herbert Brodkin Productions; Titus Productions.

Executive producer: Herbert Brodkin
Supervising producer: Robert 'Buzz' Berger
Producer: Thomas DeWolfe, Eugene O'Neill Memorial Theatre Center
Director: Claudia Weill
Teleplay: Kathleen Betsko Yale

Cast: Dewuhurst (Marie Kovacs), Jason Robards (Stephen Kovacs), Peter MacNicol (Joe Kovacs), Kathy Bates (Katrine Kovacs), Suzanna Hamilton (Iris Kovacs, Bill Cobbs (Wiggins),Tom Wright (Paulie), Thomas Martell Brimm (Stoop), Daniel R. Butler (Buddy Zupnik), Richard Cowl (Janos), E. Brian Dean (Sneaky Pete), Cherie Elledge (Elvira Mae), Pat Fuleihan (Vee), Don Jones (Immigration Officer), Becky Jordan (Unemployment Clerk), Dan Lauria (Skuska)

A Cockney girl comes to America to join the young soldier-husband she met when he was stationed in England. She ends up in a distressed mining town in the home of his parents (Dewhurst and Robards).

(See A50.)

P87   As Is. Showtime July 27, 1986. Brandman Productions; Interchange Television Group.

Executive producer: Michael Brandman
Producer: Iris Merlis
Co-producer: Patrick Whitley

Director: Michael Lindsay-Hogg
Teleplay: William M. Hoffman
From the play by: Hoffman

Cast: Dewhurst (Hospice Worker), Robert Carradine (Rich Farrell), Jonathan Hadary (Saul), Joanna Miles (Lily), Allan Scarfe (Brother), Julie Ganton (Brother's Wife), Doug Annear (Chet), Samantha Langevin (Partner), Reg Dreger (1st Doctor), Gerald Lenton (2nd Doctor), Tonya Williams (TV Commentator), Jeremy Ratchford (1st Pickup), Chris Owens (2nd Pickup), Andrew Lewarne (1st Clone), Ted Dillon (2nd Clone), Robbie Haas (Bartender), Stuart Arnot (1st Man), Linda Kash (1st Woman), Margaret Bard (2nd Woman), Brian Young (1st person with AIDS), Paddy Campanaro (2nd person with AIDS), Leonard Chow (3rd person with AIDS), Elizabeth Rukavina (Nurse), Jason Blicker (Hospital Worker), Robert Morelli (1st Dealer), Billie Newton Davis (2nd Dealer)

A former lover returns to care for his homosexual lover who is stricken with AIDS in this made-for-cable film version of the 1985 Broadway play..

P88   Sword of Gideon. HBO November 29, 1986 Alliance Entertainment Corporation; CTV Television Network; HBO Pictures; Telefilm Canada; Rogers Cablesystems; Societe Radio-Canada; Films Ariane (France)

Executive producer: John Kemeny, Denis Heroux
Producer: Robert Lantos
Director: Michael Anderson
Teleplay: Chris Bryant
From the book Vengeance by: George Jonas

Cast: Dewhurst (Golda Meir), Steven Bauer (Avner), Robert Joy (Hans), Leslie Hope (Shoshana), Laurent Malet (Jean), Peter Dvorsky (Carl), Rod Steiger (Mordechai Samuels), Michael York (Robert), John Hirsch (Avner's Father), Linda Griffiths (Miriam), Lino Ventura (Papa), Cyrielle Claire (Jeanette Von Lesseps), Eric Gaudry (Louis), Audi Levy (major General Harrai), Hrant Alianak (Wael Zwaiter), Miro Wahba (Mahmoud Hamshari), Daniel Alfie (Ali Hassan Salameh), Neil Kroetch (Abu Daoud), Sonia Benezra (Mrs. Hamshari); With: Septimiu Sever, Gregory Tal, Arthur Grosser, Danette Mackay, Israel Rubinchik, Shawn Laurence, Carolanne Francis, Serge Bossac, Nati Dabakh, Mimi D'Estee,

Pierre Zimmer, Pauline Rathbone, Harry Hill, Jack Messenger, Gladys Hadaya, Pierre Magny, Ernesto Echevarria, Bassir Dany Rajjab, David Weinstein, Clare Walker

Dewhurst turns up periodically in this action adventure about global vengeance and a secret anti-terrorist team sent to investigate those responsible for the 1972 Munich Olympics massacre.

(See A49, A51, A52.)

1987

P89   The Longest Hurrah. WMHT-TV (Schenectady, N.Y.) February 25, 1987.

Executive producer: Dick Hoffman
Producer, director: Steve Dunn

Narrator: Dewhurst

This telefilm documents the birth and growth of the political machine that remains alive in the city and county of Albany, N.Y. It focuses on Dan O'Connell, who had been mayor of the capital city for 42 years when he died in 1983, and on his protege, Erastus Corning, 2nd.

Review: Variety (March 11, 1987).

P90   Bigfoot. ABC March 25, 1987. Walt Disney TV. Disney Sunday Movie.

Producer: Michael S. McLean
Director: Danny Huston
Teleplay by: John Groves

Cast: Dewhurst, James Sloyan, Gracie Harrison, Joseph Maher, Adam Kare, Candice Cameron, Bernie White, Dawan Scott, Jerry Chambers

Dewhurst, as a scientist, works to save animals from a wicked hunter.

(See A54.)

P91   Anne of Avonlea: The Continuing Story of Anne of Green Gables
      (a.k.a Anne of Green Gables: The Sequel) (series). The Disney
      Channel. May 19 & 26, June 2 & 9, 1987. Sullivan Films of
      Toronto, The Disney Channel, PBS's Wonder Works, Canadian
      Broadcasting Co. & Telefilm Canada.

      Executive producer: Kevin Sullivan
      Director: Sullivan
      Teleplay by: Sullivan
      Based on the books by: Lucy Maud Montgomery

      Cast: Dewhurst (Marilla Cuthbert), Megan Follows (Anne), Patricia
      Hamilton (Rachel Lynde), Jonathan Crombie, Schuyler Grant,
      Frank Converse, Marilyn Lightstone, Rosemary Dunsmore,
      Genevieve Appleton, Suzanne Hoffman, Wendy Hiller, Les Carlson,
      Mag Ruffman, Kay Hawtrey, David Fox, David Hughes, Charmion
      King, Rosemary Radcliffe, Robert Collins, Kate Lynch, Charles
      Joliffe, Nuala Fitzgerald, Jacqueline Blais, Bruce McCollogh, Anna
      Ferguson, Miranda de Pencier, Patty Carroll Brown, Chick Roberts,
      Trish Nettleton, Ian Heath, Larry Aubrey, Jennifer Inch, Zach
      Ward, Morgan Chapman, Sheila Harcourt, Janice Bryan, Dora
      Dainton, America Weston, Kathryn Trainor, Brigit Wilson, Martin
      Donlevy, Molly McNeil, Juno Mills-Cockell, Dave Foley, Marilyn
      Boyle, Araby Lockhart, Lynne Gorman, Maxine Miller, Meg
      Hogarth, Carolyn Hetherington, Robert Galbraith, Michael Fletcher,
      Gladys O'Connor, Glori Gage, Fred Booker, Ingrid Bauer, Louise
      Nichol

      Anne (Megan Follows) flirts with adulthood in her individualistic
      manner. The film is set in Canada's Prince Edward Island circa
      1909.

      Review: Variety (June 10, 1987).

      (See also A55, A76.)

                              1989

P92   Those She Left Behind. NBC March 6, 1989. NBC Productions.

      Producer: R.W. Goodwin
      Director: Waris Hussein
      Teleplay by: Michael O'Hara

Cast: Dewhurst (Margaret Page), Gary Cole (Scott Grimes), Mary Page Keller (Sue Grimes), Joanne Kerns (Diane Pappas)

Realtor Scott Grimes is devastated when he loses his wife in childbirth. He is left to raise his daughter, Katie. Scott and mother-in-law (Dewhurst) are reconciled through their mutual loss.

Reviews:
Los Angeles Times (March 6, 1989)
The New York Times (March 6, 1989).

(See also A71.)

P93   Lantern Hill. CBC December 30, 1990. Sullivan Films of Toronto in association with CBC-TV and the Disney Channel.

Executive producer: Trudy Grant
Producer, director: Kevin Sullivan
Teleplay by: Fiona McHugh, Sullivan
Based on the novel, Jane of Lantern Hill, by:
Lucy Maud Montgomery

Cast: Dewhurst (the housekeeper), Sam Waterston (the father), Marion Bennett (the young girl), Zoe Caldwell (the mother), Sarah Polley (the young girl's friend), Patricia Phillips, Vivian Reis, Joyce Champion, Florence Paterson, Robert Benson, Sharry Flett .

Set in 1935, this telefilm is a compelling family tale about the supernatural and family reconciliation.

Review: Variety (January 21, 1991).

TELEVISION EPISODES, SERIES, SPECIALS

P94 Dupont Show of the Month episode. The Count of Monte Cristo. October 28, 1958. CBS.

P95 U.S. Steel Hour episode. The Hours Before Dawn (episode). U.S. Steel Hour. September 23, 1959. CBS.

P96 How Long the Night (special). September 30, 1959. NN (Non Network).

P97 Play of the Week episode. Medea. NN October 12, 1959.

P98 Play of the Week episode. Burning Bright. NN October 26, 1959.

P99 Dupont Show of the Month episode. I, Don Quixote. CBS November 9, 1959.

P100 Ben Casey episode. I Remember a Lemon Tree. ABC October 23, 1961.

P101 Focus episode. NBC January 21, 1962. An adaptation of Arthur Miller's novel.

P102 The Nurses episode. The Fly Shadow. CBS October 11, 1962.

P103 Eleventh Hour episode. I Don't Belong in a White-Painted House. NBC October 24, 1962.

P104 U.S. Steel Hour episode. Night Run to the West. CBS February 20, 1963.

P105 Dupont Show of the Month episode. Something to Hide. NBC May 5, 1963.

P106 East Side/West Side episode. <u>Nothing But the Half Truth</u>. CBS March 30, 1964.

P107 Dr. Kildare episode. <u>All Brides Should Be Beautiful</u>. NBC March 11, 1965.

P108 The Virginian episode. <u>The Executioners</u>. NBC April 28, 1965.

P109 Alfred Hitchcock Hour episode. <u>Night Fever</u>. NBC May 2, 1965.

P110 The FBI episode. <u>The Baby Sitter</u>. ABC February 13, 1966.

P111 Play of the Week episode. <u>Burning Bright</u>. NN October 19, 1966.

P112 The Big Valley episode. <u>A Day of Terror</u>. ABC December 12, 1966.

P113 <u>My Mother's House</u> (special). NN May 7, 1967.

P114 NET Playhouse episode. <u>My Mother's House</u>. PBS February 17, 1972.

P115 You Are There episode <u>The Trial of Susan B. Anthony</u>. CBS March 25, 1972.

P116 Wide World of Mystery episode. <u>A Prowler in the Heat</u>. ABC March 26, 1973.

P117 <u>Portrait: Legend in Granite</u> (special). ABC December 14, 1973.

P118 Three Women Alone (special). NN (a.k.a. syndicated: program made for non-network use) June 2, 1974.

(See A12.)

P119 Quincy, M.E., episode. For Love of Joshua. NBC February 3, 1982.

P120 Great Performances episode. PBS Alice in Wonderland. October 3, 1983.

P121 You Can't Take It With You (special). SHO May 1984.

P122 Finder of Lost Loves episode. Echoes. ABC October 27, 1984.

P123 The Love Boat episode. The Death and Life of Sir Albert Demerest. ABC November 24, 1984.

P124 An American Portrait episode. Julia Lathrop. CBS May 28, 1986.

P125 Tennessee Williams' South (special). A&E April 7, 1987.

P126 New Twilight Zone episode. There Was an Old Woman. NN (a.k.a. syndicated: program made for non-network use) December 17, 1988.

P127 Short Stories episode. Woman in the Wind. A&E January 9, 1989.

P128 Murphy Brown episode. Mama Said. CBS March 6, 1989. (Other episodes, as well. Dewhurst appeared as Murphy's mother for three seasons.)

(See 17, A69, A151.)

Writings about Dewhurst and Her Productions

BOOKS AND PERIODICAL ARTICLES

1956

A1   "Taming of the Shrew." Variety (August 1956).

In this Shakespeare Theatre Workshop performance, Dewhurst gives a robust performance as Katharine.

1957

A2   "Stage for Two." Theatre Arts (April 57).

Colleen Dewhurst and Bryarly Lee, both having made their debuts on Broadway after winning acclaim in Off-Broadway productions, will be appearing in leading roles in Paul Osborn's new comedy Maiden Voyage.

1958

A3   "Jose Quintero's Children of Darkness." Cue (March 15, 1958).

In this gem of a drama, Dewhurst plays the role of a lusty wench. The reviewer says that she speaks the English language with a clarity and gusto few can equal.

1959

A4   Hewes, Henry. "Antony and Cleopatra at the Heckscher Theatre."
Saturday Review 42 (January 31, 1959): 24-5.

Mr. Scott's Antony seems completely impervious to Cleopatra's
charms and more concerned with his own ego. Dewhurst's
problems stem in good part from having to play opposite this
conception of Antony. A *femme fatale* whose stuff is not having
any effect is hardly a *femme fatale*.

1963

A5   Oliver, Edith. "Off Broadway: O'Neill on Bleecker Street." New
Yorker (January 19, 1963).

In Desire Under the Elms, Dewhurst gives a marvelous
performance as she changes from a woman whose surface calm is
a mask for repugnance and cunning.

A6   Pryce-Jones, Alan. "Cleo in the Park." Theatre Arts (July 1963):
16+.

The interview takes place during a rehearsal break from Antony
and Cleopatra. Dewhurst loves the play--"the way it evolves from
a love affair to a kind of terrible marriage." She talks of her past
roles, which have had a cumulative effect in her being type-cast
as a "heavy."

A7   Smith, Michael. "Self-Involved Nuts in Guise Of Actors--Not the
Scotts." The Village Voice (May 30, 1963).

Obie Award winners Dewhurst and Scott (Desire Under the Elms)
make themselves available for interviews, Dewhurst at the
Delacorte where she is rehearsing Antony and Cleopatra, Scott at the
sound stage of the old Biograph Studios in the Bronx, where he is
filming East Side, West Side. As for the O'Neill play, Dewhurst
thinks the part of Abbie was almost written for her.

1965

A8   Hewes, Henry. "A Moon for the Misbegotten." Saturday Review
      (October 23, 1965). A theatre review.

      Buffalo's Studio Arena Theatre, which has been converted from a
      community theatre to a professional nonprofit enterprise, has
      opened with a performance of A Moon for the Misbegotten.
      Despite the shortcomings attributed to a lack of rehearsal time,
      Dewhurst rises to magnificent moments in the role of Josie.

A9   Vaughan, Stuart. A Possible Theatre: The Experiences of a
      Pioneer Director in America's Resident Theatre! New York:
      McGraw-Hill, 1965. 33-87.

      Vaughan, who directed the Papp's Shakespeare Workshop
      productions from 1956-59, writes of his experiences, which include
      references to Dewhurst's performance in The Taming of the Shrew.

1972

A10 "The Awful Truth." Variety (November 15, 1972).

      As guest speaker at the annual Edwin Booth birthday luncheon at
      The Players Club, Dewhurst told of her early attempts to get into
      the theatre. Her grandmother, who considered a career on the stage
      shocking, died without ever knowing about Dewhurst's success.

1974

A11 Kalem, T.E. "Gorgeous Gael." Time (January 21, 1974).

      Dewhurst and her leading man Jason Robards were not expecting
      the thunderous reception that greeted A Moon for the Misbegotten
      on Broadway. The tall and handsome, voluptuous figured
      Dewhurst, according to the reviewer, is well-suited to the O'Neill's
      full-blooded Earth Mother conception of women.

A12 Mermey, Joanna. "Colleen Dewhurst." The Village Voice (June 6,
      1974): 102 A television review.

Dewhurst narrates WOR-TV's Three Women Alone. The show examines the lives of three women, a 35-year-old photographer, a 29-year-old advertising executive, and a 50-year-old widow from Westport, Connecticut.

1975

A13 Stone, Judy. "An Interview with Actress Colleen Dewhurst." Playgirl (April 1975): 48, 89, 118.

The interview took place in the kitchen of the actress's rented beach house. Dewhurst voiced her opinions on the women's movement. Mothers must encourage their daughters to fulfill themselves in ways other than marriage.

1976

A14 Warhol, Andy. "Colleen Dewhurst." Interview (August 1976): 17, 19.

Warhol interviewed Dewhurst after an evening's performance in Who's Afraid of Virginia Woolf? He asked why she broke into uncontrollable laughter after she delivering the line "Some people feed on the calamity of others." (It took two lines, several rounds of encouraging applause and a full minute for the actress to regain her composure.) She explained that she had given up cigarettes, and onstage the line was interpreted as a reference to the problem she was having. The interview continued over supper at the Algonquin, where Dewhurst stays when she is in town.

1977

A15 Clurman, Harold. "An Almost Perfect Person." Nation 225 (November 19, 1977): 540. A theatre review.

The trouble with the play is that it is conceived along conventional lines of a sub-Simon or Kaufman script. The show's asset is the "excellent actress Colleen Dewhurst, one of the most truly womanly . . . and wise players on Broadway's boards today."

A16 Goodman, Walter. "On Stage: Theatrical Stunts." New Leader 60
(November 21, 1977): 23. A theatre review.

Dewhurst brings her notable talents to An Almost Perfect Person, a
vehicle that "leaves her stranded."

1979

A17 Deford, Frank. "Ice Castles." Sports Illustrated 50 (March 26,
1979): 49. A film review.

In this "most pretentious of the new Rocky rip-offs," neither
Dewhurst nor Skerritt appear to have the foggiest notion what the
turgid script is saying to them.

A18 "Colleen Dewhurst: Champion for Women." Screen Actor (Fall
1979).

Dewhurst met with members of the New York Screen Actors'
Guild to voice her support of the October 10 protest rally against
the quantity and quality of roles for women and minorities. She
sees public awareness as the only answer.

A19 "Ice Castles." Christian Century 96 (February 28, 1979): 228. A
film review.

Dewhurst in the role of coach/adviser gives one of her "robust
earthmother performances" in a movie that is unabashedly
sentimental.

A20 Oliver, Edith. "Off-Broadway: Waiting at the Church." New
Yorker 55 (March 12, 1979): 108. A theatre review.

Dewhurst, since replaced by Nancy Marchand in Taken in
Marriage, portrayed well the crusty mother in her belief in loyalty
and fidelity.

A21 Simon, John. "Theater: Triumphs for the Will." New York 12
(March 26, 1979): 95. A theatre review.

At moments Taken in Marriage lights up destructively but amusingly. Dewhurst could not be better as the mother.

A22 "Picks & Pans: Screen: When a Stranger Calls." People Weekly 12 (October 15, 1979): 24. A film review.

Durning and Dewhurst are adept as obsessed ex-cop and barfly who team with the police to trap a menacing telephone caller.

1980

A23 Freeman, Don. "TV Previews." The San Diego Union (January 21, 1980): B8.

Dewhurst is starring in Death Penalty on NBC-TV. Her career has been devoted to the stage, but lately she has turned her eyes to Hollywood to make money.

A24 Kauffmann, Stanley. "Tribute." New Republic 183 (December 27, 1980): 24. A moving-picture review.

Tribute needs a good director. Dewhurst is a melancholy reminder of the young woman who had a chance to be great actor.

1981

A25 Crute, Sheree. "Good News For Our Lives After 40...50...60." Ms 10 (August 1, 1981): 48.

Dewhurst has her friends, her sons, an enjoyable relationship with their father. All she needs, she says, is a good acting role to be totally happy.

A26 "Ned and Jack." Variety (November 11, 1981): 84. A theatre review.

Dewhurst has staged Ned and Jack at the Little Theatre. Theatre history buffs are most likely to be attracted to and engrossed by the comedy-drama about the celebrated actor John Barrymore and actor Edward Sheldon.

A27 "On the Program." <u>School Library Journal</u> 27 (April 1981): 19.

Library advocate Dewhurst will be the guest speaker at the Library
Association Conference to be held at the Ryetown Hilton,
Port Chester, NY.

A28 Simon, John. "<u>Ned and Jack</u>." <u>New York</u> 14 (June 1, 1981): 45. A
theatre review.

Dewhurst has directed the show with a "desperate busyness that
more than often trips up the meaning of the play."

A29 Simon, John. "Theater: <u>Ned and Jack</u>." <u>New York</u> 14
(November 23, 1981): 87.

There is no compelling reason to have written this play. The author
has done rewrites. Dewhurst has pushed the actors harder, but it is
a "bafflement." It should never have been transferred from Off-
Broadway.

1982

A30 Brustein, Robert. "Great Ladies and Others: <u>The Queen and the
Rebels</u>." <u>New Republic</u> 187 (November 1, 1982): 25. A review.

Dewhurst is always a warm and cordial presence, but there is little
in her presence to justify reviving the play.

A31 Eckard, Bonnie Jean. <u>Camille in America</u> (Dumas, France.
<u>University of Denver</u> (0061), 1982. UMI No. AAC8315896.
A dissertation.

Alexander Dumas fils's <u>Camille</u> was one of the most popular
vehicles for actresses performing in America during the last half of
the nineteenth century. Chapter Eleven, entitled "The Demise of
Camille," includes a performance by Colleen Dewhurst.

A32 Gill, Brendan. "The Theatre: Pinchbeck Profundities."
<u>New Yorker</u> 58 (October 11, 1982): 156. A theatre review.

The cast of The Queen and the Rebels, headed by Dewhurst, is competent. Yet, despite their efforts, the play has an implausible ring.

A33 Morrison, Joelle. "Colleen Dewhurst: The Actor As Director." East Side Express (June 11, 1981): 6.

After 20 years of working Off and Off-Off Broadway, then in films, Dewhurst returns to Off-Off Broadway to direct her first play, Ned and Jack. During the interview onstage at the Hudson Guild Theatre, she reveals her initial love of the play, her working relationship with the playwright, and her opinion that the production merits a transfer, as is, to Broadway.

A34 "The Queen and the Rebels." Variety (October 6, 1982): 105. A theatre review.

Dewhurst's big performance is vigorous, emotionally charged, and fully satisfying. She is "properly hardbitten in the early scenes, then funny and sardonic as she teases the rebels . . . She's just about the whole show."

A35 Sauvage, Leo. "On Stage: Poets on Broadway." New Leader 67 (November 1982): 17. A theatre review.

The Queen and the Rebels is winning plaudits for Dewhurst. Argia, the prostitute, is endowed by the actress with an awesome dramatic presence.

A36 Simon, John. "Theater: A Queen for a Night?" New York 15 (October 11, 1982): 83. A theatre review.

In the Queen and the Rebels Dewhurst "performs with dignity a juicy jollity and an earthy savor that contains a bit of infinity."

A37 Weales, Gerald. "Stage: Triumph of the Word: Belle on Broadway." The Queen and the Rebels." Commonweal 109 (November 19, 1982): 625. A theatre review.

In The Queen and the Rebels Dewhurst shows us the many faces that belong to Argia. Her powerful reading shows that a good play can give body to alternate truth.

1983

A38 "Picks & Pans: Etc.: Willa Cather: A Look of Remembrance." People Weekly 19 (May 9, 1983): 28. A radio review.

In the first section of a National Public Radio three-part radio series, Dewhurst reads selections from the autobiographical My Antonia about the Great Plains novelist. Dewhurst's voice "rings like rolling thunder," but loses its effectiveness when director Joan Micklin Silver adds "florid" background music.

A39 "Chatter." People Weekly 19 (May 16, 1983): 130.

At a benefit for Save the Theatres, a group formed to preserve Broadway stages threatened by developers, Dewhurst recalled a 1974 performance of A Moon for the Misbegotten that required her to sit quietly on stage for three minutes.

A 40 Cullen, Bernadette J. "Residents Agree to Take the Cake." Chelsea Clinton News (October 6, 1983): 1, 8.

Dewhurst spoke to a lunchtime crowd of more than three hundred mid-town office workers at a cake-sale rally held at Byrant Park to protest President Reagan's economic policies. Spearheaded by the Democracy Project and the New York Public Information Research Group, the first, national "Let Them Eat Cake" sale was held in 150 cities.

A41 Gill, Brendan. "You Can't Take It with You." New Yorker 59 (April 18, 1983): 132. A theatre review.

The present revival is irresistible even with its flaws. The distinguished cast includes Dewhurst as the Grand Duchess.

1984

A42 Burmester, David. "Short Stories on Film: Split Cherry Tree."
English Journal 73 (February 1984): 109. A film review.

The performance by Dewhurst is restrained, but powerful in the
film that promises to be as much a classroom classic as the short
story from which it was adapted.

A43 "Rainsnakes." Variety (November 28, 1984): 102.
A theatre review.

The Long Wharf Theatre (New Haven, CT.) presentation is
splendid vehicle for Dewhurst's talents.

A44 "Wisc. Hall of Fame For Hagen, Dewhurst." Variety (October 24,
1984): 441.

Actresses Uta Hagen and Colleen Dewhurst were inducted into the
Wisconsin Performing Artists Hall of Fame. They are the second
pair of performers to be so honored. The Hall of Fame was
launched in 1983 with the inductions of Dennis Morgan and Jack
Carson.

1985

A45 "Burstyn Steps Down As Equity President: Dewhurst's in Line."
Variety (February 20, 1985): 1.

The Equity nominating committee lists Dewhurst in the president
slot.

A46 "Dewhurst, Unopposed Elected Equity Prez." Variety (June 5,
1985): 83.

Dewhurst, a councillor since 1983, succeeds Ellen Burstyn, who did
not run for a second term. She was not opposed for the top elective
job and received 6,580 votes.

A47 MacKay, Gillian. "Television: Bringing a Classic to the Screen: Anne of Green Gables, CBC, Dec. 1, 2." Maclean's 98 (December 2, 1985): 78. A television review.

The regal, gravel-voiced Dewhurst makes a remarkable Marilla. Her presence is powerful.

A48 Stein, Jerry. "Cincinnati." Variety (December 4, 1985).

Dewhurst, president of the Actor's Equity Association, spoke at the fall conference of the League of Regional Theatres in Cincinnati. She called for a breakthrough in racial and ethnic barriers in casting.

1986

A49 Bemrose, John. "Television: Bittersweet Vengeance: Sword of Gileon." Maclean's 99 (December 1, 1986): 73. A television review.

Dewhurst plays a grandmotherly figure in an escapist entertainment that rates nine out of ten.

A50 Jarvis, Jeff. "Picks & Pans: Tube: Johnny Bull." People Weekly 25 (May 19, 1986): 9. A television review.

Jarvis feels that it is worth watching at least two-thirds of the program to enjoy Dewhurst, Hamilton, and Bates.

A51 ------------. "Picks & Pans: Tube: Sword of Gideon." People Weekly 25 (December 1, 1986): 11. A television review.

Dewhurst is Golda in a telefilm that starts with a good idea, but suffers from a bad script and poor directing.

A52 Leonard, John. "Sword of Gideon." New York 19 (December 1, 1986): 140. A television review.

HBO tells us in the scroll at the end of the film that the world is still looking for a "civilized response" to terror. Leonard believes this as much as he believes Dewhurst as Golda Meir.

A53 "Tribute to Dewhurst To Benefit Long Wharf." Variety (July 16, 1986): 119.

Dewhurst is honored for her many contributions to the American theatre and as president of Actors' Equity Association. The proceeds of the event will go toward the Long Wharf Theatre's National Endowment for the Arts Challenge Grant.

1987

A54 Jarvis, Jeff. "Picks & Pans: Bigfoot." People Weekly 27 (March 9, 1987): 11. A television review.

In one of Disney's better films, the actress portrays a scientist who teams with parents and their children to save animals from an evil hunter.

A55 Johnson, Brian. "Anne of Green Gables--the Sequel." Maclean's 100 (December 7, 1987): 46A. A television review.

The show breathes life into an enduring legend with a magical performance by Dewhurst.

A56 Jones, Kenneth W. "Living Double Lives." School Library Journal 37 (December 1987). A 16mm film review.

Dewhurst narrates the twenty-seven minute film which suggests that the public can influence the use and spread of nuclear weapons. The film is produced by Film Ideas. It is also available on videocassette. Recommended grade 7 and up.

A57 Mano, D. Keith. "Colleen Dewhurst; As Large in Laughter as in Passionate Presence, Her Hunger For Life Remains Vast and Unsatisfied." People Weekly 27 (March 9, 1987): 80.

In this biographical profile Dewhurst talks about her current role in
My Gene, her home in the country, her sons Alexander, 26,
Campbell, 25, and her relationship with Ken Marsolais.

A58 Radin, Victoria. "Theater: Scenes from a Marriage." Vogue 177
(January 1987): 38.

Dewhurst and playwright Barbara Gelb will tell Mrs. Eugene
O'Neill's side of the story in My Gene, which is to open at the
Public Theater this month. Dewhurst is mentioned in passing in the
Gelb interview.

A59 Simon, John. "Theater: My Gene." New York 20 (February 9,
1987): 56. A theatre review.

Dewhurst interprets her jumbled data and quotations, "including
such improbable mnemonic feats as labeling of events with their
exact year, month, day, and hour," with restrained intensity and
bouncy good humor. She "picks a steadfast, purposeful way through
a maze of pitfalls."

1988

A60 "Ah, Wilderness!." Variety (June 29, 1988): 65. A theatre review.

Dewhurst is delightful as the fusspot mother, a softhearted
matriarch who keeps the household together.

A61 "Dewhurst Returned, Colton Is Defeated in Equity Voting." Variety
(June 8, 1988): 75.

Dewhurst was reelected president of Actors Equity Association.
This is a second three-year-term for Dewhurst.

A62 Hersh, Amy. "Colleen Dewhurst: At Home with the O'Neills."
TheaterWeek (June 20, 1988): 8-11.

The celebrated actress comes to terms with a great playwright's
contrasting visions of woman as matriarch. The First International
Festival of the Arts brings Dewhurst back on Broadway for a

limited engagement in <u>Long Day's Journey Into Night</u> and <u>Ah, Wilderness!</u> ,which will be presented in repertory for the O'Neill centennial. Dewhurst finds it a relief to alternate the relentless intensity of O'Neill's tragedy with the upbeat piece.

A63 "<u>Long Day's Journey into Night</u>." <u>Variety</u> (June 22, 1988): 70. A theatre review.

Dewhurst's absorbingly crafted reading of Mary Tyrone comes over more directly than in previous productions. She adds a hitherto mostly latent feminist color to the play.

A64 Oliver, Edith. "<u>Ah, Wilderness!</u> " <u>New Yorker</u> 64 (July 4, 1988): 60. A theatre review.

The sunny revival features Robards and Dewhurst with smiles on their faces.

A65 -------------. "<u>Long Day's Journey into Night</u>." <u>New Yorker</u> 64 (July 4, 1988): 59. A theatre review.

Haunted by memories of distinguished performances of the past, the reviewer finds the leads disappointing.

A66 Seibert, Gary. "Theater: The Tragic and the Comic." <u>America</u> 159 (July 23, 1988): 64. A theatre review.

Dewhurst gives <u>A Long Day's Journey</u> its focus, as does her Essie Miller of <u>Ah, Wilderness!</u> She commands the stage even when she is not on it.

A67 Simon, John. "<u>Ah, Wilderness!</u>/ <u>Long Day's Journey into Night</u>." <u>New York</u> 21 (July 11, 1988): 48. A theatre review.

In <u>Ah, Wilderness!</u> Dewhurst performs well as Essie, the mother, with the proper timing and emphasis. As for <u>Long Day's Journey into Night</u>, nothing quite works. She gets off to a good start, but shows no vulnerability in her collapse in the final scene.

A68 Sweeting, Paul and John Zinsser. "The Isak Dinesen Collection."
Publishers Weekly 234 (November 4, 1988): 56. Audio-tape
reviews.

Four unabridged stories are read by Dewhurst and Julie Harris on
five cassettes for Audio Partners. Dewhurst's rendering of
"Babette's Feast" has the quality of a "rough caress." Its visceral
impact weaves the recurring themes of love and lost opportunity
into a "resplendent fabric."

1989

A69 Buckley, Michael. "An Interview With Colleen Dewhurst."
TheaterWeek (October 1989): 34-35.

Associating her with the works by O'Neill, Albee, and Shakespeare,
audiences seem surprised to find Dewhurst performing in a
comedy--as they were when she played Candice Bergen's mother
on the CBS-TV sitcom, Murphy Brown. Dewhurst speaks of
various roles she's played throughout her career and acknowledges
the great writers like Albee and O'Neill who insist that the actor
capture the moment.

A70 Cozzone, Camille. "Taking the Stage: Colleen Dewhurst."
Harper's Bazaar 122 (August 1989) 153, 188.

The actress is profiled. Dewhurst, as president of the Actors'
Equity Association, is the spokesperson for a vision of a national
theatre. She is saddened because theatre has become elitist.

A71 Jarvis, Jeff. "Picks & Pans: Those She Left Behind."
People Weekly 31 (March 6, 1989): 14. A television review.

Jarvis only mentions that Dewhurst plays the role of the stern
mother-in-law.

A72 Morehouse, Rebecca. "A Theatregoer's Notebook: Goldstar Tony
Award Performances." Playbill (May 1989): 24.

O'Neill's A Moon for the Misbegotten raised Dewhurst to stardom
and a Tony Award after twenty-five years of acting. Dewhurst

remembers the days of making the rounds, finding no-nothing parts, and "going out and drinking tea."

A73 "Pitt's Kaufman Award to Dewhurst." Variety (November 15, 1989): 15.

Dewhurst became the third recipient of Pittsburgh Public Theatre's George S. Kaufman Award for lifetime achievement in the theatre. Kaufman's daughter, Anne Kaufman Schneider, presented the award.

A74 Thompson, Frank. "See These and Weep: For Crying Out Loud, It's Hard to Beat these Tearjerkers: Anne of Green Gables." American Film 15 (December 1989):68. A video recording review.

Dewhurst role as the spinster Marilla Cuthbert is captured on this Buena Vista home video.

1990

A75 ----------------. "Video Classics: The Nun's Story." American Film 15 (May 20, 1990): 56. A video recording review.

Dewhurst is cast in a supporting role in this austere and restrained meditation on the spiritual struggles of a Belgian nun, played by Audrey Hepburn. A Warner Home video.

A76 Turbide, Diane. "Television: Anne's Home Town." Maclean's 103 (January 8, 1990): 42. A television review.

A new $15 million series returns to idyllic Avonlea. The lavish thirteen-part series is one of the most expensive television productions ever mounted in Canada. Dewhurst and Patricia Hamilton, perfect foils for each other in Anne of Green Gables, return to their roles in the sequel, Anne of Avonlea, as the upright Marilla Cuthbert and the busybody Rachel Lynde.

1991

A77 "Colleen Dewhurst." Variety (August 26, 1991): 98.

The obituary recalls the career of one of the great stage actresses of her generation, an interpreter without equal of Eugene O'Neill.

A78   Feingold, Michael. "Colleen Dewhurst, 1924-91." Village Voice 36 (September 3, 1991): 94, 95.

The grandeur of Dewhurst is the focus of this obituary. She is remembered as a stage presence so powerful that her characters, particularly in the O'Neill plays, seemed to represent nature itself.

A79   Gardner, Jeff. "A View from the Audience: Colleen Dewhurst 1924-1991." Playbill (October 1991): 70.

A vignette, written about Dewhurst by a young acting student, emphasizes the star's renowned generosity and serves as a fitting memorial to the actress. During a difficult scene the actor passed an imaginary glass of water to Dewhurst in a scene they shared. "Thanks, the water was helpful," Dewhurst responded at the end of the day.

A80   Goodman, Mark and Ann Guerin. "Brava, Colleen." People Weekly 36 (September 9, 1991): 53-54.

This is another obituary that mentions the important events in Dewhurst's career.

A81   La Rue, Michele. "Dewhurst's "Remembrance": Laughing through Tears." Backstage (September 27, 1991): 1, 6.

A two hour "Remembrance" for Dewhurst was held at the Martin Beck Theatre on September 23. Her laughter set the tone for the memorial. Invoked by her associates on stage, it was echoed on film clips during the closing moments.

A82   McNally, Terrence. "The Importance of Being Hirschfelded." The New York Times Book Review (December 1, 1991): 14.

McNally will always remember the Colleen Dewhurst who is found on page 252 of Al Hirschfeld's book of drawings. The artist has drawn Dewhurst in what proved to be her last Broadway appearance, as Essie Miller in <u>Ah, Wilderness!</u>

A83 Novak, Ralph. "<u>Dying Young</u>." <u>People Weekly</u> 35 (July 1, 1991): 13.

Dewhurst overcomes "an embarrassing tea-leaf reading scene" to create an appealing presence. She plays the owner of a winery.

A84 Simon, John. "<u>Elektra</u>." <u>New York</u> 24 (March 25, 1991): 70. An opera review.

Before a concert performance of Richard Strauss's <u>Elektra</u> by the Vienna Philharmonic, conducted by Lorin Maazel at Carnegie Hall, Dewhurst was a sensible yet feeling Elektra in a reading of Hofmannsthal's libretto.

A85 Stuart, Otis. "American Classic: Colleen Dewhurst, 1926-91." <u>Lincoln Center Stagebill</u> (November 1991): 50.

An homage is paid to Dewhurst, whose career began in the classics. She played Lady Macbeth, Cleopatra, and Camille, and called herself the "revival girl" early in her career. She crowned her career in a contemporary repertory of American theatre's own brand of classicism in the plays of Albee and O'Neill.

A86 Walsh, Thomas. "Colleen Dewhurst 1924-1991." <u>Backstage</u> (August 30, 1991): 1, 5.

The obituary is written in appreciation of the celebrated actress. Dewhurst's forty-year career is highlighted.

NEWSPAPER ARTICLES

1956

A87 Watts, Richard, Jr. "Two on the Aisle: Random Notes on This and That." New York Post (September 25, 1956).

A young actress worth watching is Dewhurst,who is presently performing in Camille at the Cherry Lane Theatre.

1957

A88 Watts, Richard, Jr. "Two on the Aisle: Random Notes on This and That." New York Post (August 20, 1957).

Nothing so pleasant has happened in New York as the exciting production of Macbeth in Central Park. Dewhust is an actress waiting to be discovered by a commercial producer.

1958

A89 Fischer, Muriel. "Off-Broadway Answer to Anna Magnani." New York World-Telegram and Sun (August 4, 1958).

Her hair is "undisguisedly peppered with strains of premature gray," but Dewhurst makes known her preference for the au naturel. She also prefers little makeup. As for the question of fulfillment, she tells the interviewer that without the theatre it would not be possible. Her twelve-year marriage to Vickery has recently ended. She wants to remarry and raise a family.

A90 McClain, John. "Man about Manhattan: Play Gets Second Chance." New York Journal-American (February 24, 1958).

The revival of Edwin Justin Mayer's Children of Darkness boasts of the best Off-Broadway performers. Dewhurst has the leading role.

A91 Wahls, Robert. "Women Snub Colleen for Hot Love Scene." Sunday News (April 1958).

At the beginning of her career, while performing in a stock production in Gatlinburg, Tennessee, Dewhurst was practically shunned at a tea given by ladies who seemed to have confused her with her role. Her reputation as an emotional actress has been established. She is about to stake her claim to an international reputation in O'Neill's A Moon for the Misbegotten to be presented at the Gian-Carlo Menotti Festival of Two Worlds in Spoleto, Italy, this summer.

A92 Winsten, Archer. "Rages and Outrages." New York Post (August 18, 1958).

After ten years of acting on stage in New York City, Dewhurst was approached by Fred Zinnemann to play the lead in The Nun's Story, filmed in Rome. The actress recalls the excitement of making her first movie and of her first trip abroad. She is now back in New York for the Circle in the Square production of Children of Darkness.

1959

A93 Fields, Sidney. "Only Human: First Twelve Years Are the Hardest!" Daily Mirror (March 4, 1955).

Children of Darkness has given Dewhurst recognition as an actress. She recalls the struggle, her marriage to James Vickery, their cold-water flat, her passion for a nice apartment.

1960

A94 Little, Stuart W. "Theater News: Colleen Dewhurst Wins Broadway Play's Big Role." New York Herald Tribune (September 9, 1960).

After receiving critical acclaim Off-Broadway, Dewhurst has been cast in a central role in the Broadway production of Tad Mosel's All the Way Home. Rehearsals start in October.

A95 Herridge, Frances. "Across the Footlights: Dewhurst Has Arrived on B'way." New York Post (December 23, 1960): 20.

Dewhurst plays the bereaved wife in <u>All the Way Home</u>. She has not been easy to cast because of her size and age. On the personal side, she and her new son, Alexander, and husband George C. Scott are now living in seven large rooms atop Jay Thorpe's department store, having left a Greenwich Village apartment.

1961

A96 Wahls, Robert. "Wild Colleen Is Finally Normal." <u>Sunday News</u> (January 1, 1961).

In <u>All the Way Home</u> Dewhurst has the opportunity to be a normal wife, one who adjusts to the death of her husband without becoming an alcoholic or a drug addict.

1963

A97 Fields, Sidney. "Only Human: Ballad of the Happy Colleen." <u>Daily News</u> (October 30, 1963).

Dewhurst talks about her life with husband George C. Scott, whom she calls "The Monster." They live in a spacious apartment on Riverside Drive with their two boys, Alexander, 3, and Campbell, 2. Scott is a perfectionist. When they worked together in <u>Desire Under the Elms</u>, they'd get home weary and flop into bed. She'd be dozing off, and he would get her out of bed to work on a scene. Her husband wants some land in the country, so his sons can grow up around horses.

A98 Herridge, Frances. "Across the Footlights: Lou Antonio Learns to Fight Women" <u>New York Post</u> (December 16, 1963).

Lou Antonio talks about his stage marriage to Dewhurst in <u>The Ballad of the Sad Cafe</u>. It leads to an all-out slug-fest at the end of the play. Even though a choreographer plotted the action, the fight was troublesome. They finally worked it out themselves--"mostly wrestling with a few punches." Antonio says that Dewhurst is "an amazing person to work with."

A99 Little, Stuart W. "Theater News: <u>Sad Cafe</u>." <u>New York Herald Tribune</u> (August 6, 1963).

Dewhurst will play Miss Amelia, the strong central character in The Ballad of the Sad Cafe. The role calls for a "dark, tall woman with bones and muscles like a man's"; about her face, "a tense, haggard quality."

A100 Mackin, Tom. "Mulling a 'Heavy' Fate." Newark Evening News (May 3, 1963).

Stealing a few moments from her real-life role as wife/mother and stage role in Off-Broadway production of Desire Under the Elms, Dewhurst relaxed last week at Michael's Pub on East 55th Street. When the call goes out for a "murderess," she says they send for Dewhurst. She plays the publisher who is accused of murder this Sunday in Something to Hide on NBC.

A101 Peper, William. "Colleen Dewhurst Finds Role in Sad Cafe Man-Sized Job." New York World-Telegram and The Sun (October 29, 1963).

The actress plays a mannish eccentric in the Albee play, which opens the next day. "I have no idea what people are going to think of this play. It will be interesting to see what happens," she remarks.

A102 Tallmer, Jerry. "Colleen Dewhurst Makes a Big Entrance on Broadway." New York Post (October 31, 1963).

At the opening night party for Ballad of a Sad Cafe, Dewhurst admits that husband G.C. held her hand through the entire rehearsal period. Having seen the play four times, he's home "baby-sitting with the kids."

A103 --------------. "There Is Only One Cleo to the Girl in the Park." New York Post (June 19, 1963).

While Elizabeth Taylor will perhaps get $10,000,000 for her performance in the film role of Cleopatra, Dewhurst will be paid a modest $100 a week for her stage portrayal. Dewhurst says that it's ridiculous to even compare the two salaries. Under any conditions, only the stage is important to her.

A104 Wilson, Earl. "It Happened Last Night: Revolt against Hairdressers."
New York Post (November 20, 1963).

The star of The Ballad of the Sad Cafe says that she won't let hair
appointments guide her life. Women get to be hairdo addicts. They
need their hairdos "like alcoholics need booze."

A105 Zolotow, Maurice. "Cleopatra in the Park and Home." The New
York Times (June 9, 1963).

Elizabeth Taylor is playing Cleopatra in the 20th Century-Fox film
at the same time as Dewhurst is appearing in Central Park.
Production costs and salaries are compared. When Dewhurst first
played Cleopatra in Papp's reading at the Heckscher Theatre, her
Antony was George Scott. They fell madly in love and were
married. Dewhurst sees Cleopatra as a victim of the cult of beauty,
the typical American woman who is obsessed with appearance.

1965

A106 "Who's Afraid of Mumps?" New York Post (May 28, 1965).

Dewhurst has come down with mumps while in rehearsal for a
May 31 opening of Who's Afraid of Virginia Woolf at the Bucks
County Playhouse in New Hope, Pa. Since her doctor has
determined that everyone else in the company is immune,
Dewhurst is proceeding with a degree of agony.

1967

A107 Reed, Rex. "But Colleen Almost Does." The New York Times
(November 12, 1967).

The day after the not-so-triumphant opening of More Stately
Mansions, Dewhurst says she is not sorry. She wanted to do the
play. She loves the O'Neill women.

A108 Windeler, Robert. "Colleen Dewhurst Outshines Ingrid Bergman in
O'Neill Play." The New York Times (September 14, 1967).

O'Neill's last unproduced play, More Stately Mansions, had its premiere in Los Angeles. The occasion also marked Ingrid Bergman's return to the American stage after twenty-one years. Bergman received a polite two-minute curtain call after which the audience of 2,000 cheered and applauded Dewhurst's performance with intensity.

1971

A109 Hart-Green. "Eye: Her Own Mistress." Women's Wear Daily (April 16, 1971).

Dewhurst grants an interview as All Over struggles for survival. She speaks of her roles as actress, wife, and mother. When a plays closes, she's always happy to get home.

A110 Fields, Sidney. "Only Human: Power With Words." Daily News (March 30, 1971).

In her dressing room a few days before the opening of Albee's All Over, the actress confesses her concern regarding the audience's reception of the show. She mentions her husband, George, who is never satisfied with what he does. It can make living with him difficult.

A111 Wilson, Earl. "It Happened Last Night: George C. Scotts Separated?" New York Post (May 7, 1971).

They have been married twice. Each is reported to be "very sorry it [the recent split] happened." Wilson wonders where this leaves Dewhurst's Broadway show A Definite Maybe, which Scott is supposed to direct.

1972

A112 Iachetta, Michael. "The Dark Side of Fair Colleen." Daily News (December 24, 1972).

In this profile, Dewhurst confides that she is irresponsible in many areas. She becomes bored too easily. She procrastinates. But she has a great love for people, not indiscriminate love. The only area she has complete discipline in is the theatre.

A113 The New York Times (February 3, 1972).

The Oscar-winning actor George C. Scott and his wife, the actress Colleen Dewhurst, have been divorced again. It happened first in Juarez, Mexico, in July 1965. They were married again in July 1967. Mrs. Scott obtained the second divorce in Santo Domingo, where she took advantage of the Dominican Republic's new quickie divorce law. Terms of the settlement are reported.

A114 Tallmer, Jerry. "Colleen Dewhurst: What? Shakespeare?" New York Post (July 8, 1972).

Dewhurst recalls the days at the Emmanuel Presbyterian Church on East 6th Street, talks about her current role as Gertrude, her love for divorced "G.C."

1974

A115 Beaufort, John. "Colleen Dewhurst: a Great O'Neill Heroine Come to Life." Christian Science Monitor (August 29, 1974).

In an interview backstage at the Morosco Theatre, Dewhurst expressed her amazement at success of Moon for the Misbegotten, talked about the audience responses, and analyzed the role of Josie whose "aggressiveness cloaks a sensitive romanticism."

A116 Chase, Chris. "Colleen Has Broadway Moon-Struck." The New York Times (February 17, 1974).

After twenty-seven years in theatre, the actress has her first hit in A Moon for the Misbegotten. Dewhurst reconstructs the events which led to the Broadway production. She and Quintero had done the show in 1957 in Spoleto, and in 1963 in Buffalo. They were both Moon-eager, and Jason Robards was anxious to join the team.

A117 Glover, William. "A New Diamond In Dewhurst's Crown." The Philadelphia Inquirer (February 3, 1974).

A Moon for the Misbegotten got rave reviews, and Dewhurst confesses that she is not used to seeing a line at the box office for her plays. On the personal side, she was never interested in having children. Now she's delighted. She loves people, but loves her refuge on Prince Edward Island. Would she have played for Nixon while in Washington? She thinks he should resign, but, yes, she'd play for anybody in the audience.

A118 Krebs, Albin. "Colleen Dewhurst." The New York Times (March 21, 1974).

The American Academy of Dramatic Arts will present its annual achievements award for alumni to Dewhurst, class of '47. Graduation exercises will be held on the stage of the Morosco Theatre, where the honoree is starring in A Moon for the Misbegotten.

A119 Wahls, Robert. "Footlights: Mommy Has a Hit." Sunday News (January 13, 1974).

Dewhurst has a hit with A Moon for the Misbegotten, and her boys Campbell, 12, and Alex, 14, are following her around the house chanting, "Mommy has a hit."

1975

A120 Gardella, Kay. "Television: Moon-Struck Colleen Brings Josie to TV." Daily News (May 18, 1975).

Dewhurst will recreate her Broadway role in A Moon for the Misbegotten on ABC-TV, Tuesday May 27, at 8:30 PM. She talked to Gardella about the play and the superb television direction which focuses on reaction shots. Comments were also directed to matinee ladies who prefer not to hear anything they can't understand.

A121 Thompson, Howard. "Viewpoints." The New York Times (November 25, 1975).

Dewhurst is scheduled as a guest lecturer at a discussion series at Theatre Off Park, 28 East 35th Street. She will speak about her career and the theatre.

1976

A122 Carragher, Bernard. "Personalities: Making It in Showbiz--the Hard Way." Daily News (March 28, 1976).

In an interview given at her country home, Dewhurst shares her thoughts on male-female relationships, the influence of her wonderful mother, her need for the kids, the play [Who's Afraid of Virgina Woolf?], the house--everything."

A123 Johnston, Laurie. "Notes on People: Miss Dewhurst, a Lasting Laugh." The New York Times (May 6, 1976).

The actress broke into uncontrollable and unrehearsed laughter at Tuesday night's performance of Who's Afraid of Virginia Woolf?. She related the incident to difficulties she had been having in giving up smoking while playing a role in which she had to carry a cigarette in many scenes-- and to the impishness of her fellow troupers.

A124 Pinkerton, Ann. "Eye View: TV-- or not TV?" Women's Wear Daily (August 27, 1976).

Dewhurst is thinking of going into television because it gives her six months of steady work each year. She prefers the east coast, where she feels more in control of her destiny. As for feminism, she's bored with sexual freedom and regrets that woman have managed to emasculate the opposite sex.

A125 Wilson, Earl. "It Happened Last Night: Fraternizing with the Enemy." New York Post (April 6, 1976).

Dewhurst was seen after an evening's performance of Who's Afraid of Virginia Woolf? with Ken Marsolais, one of show's producers.

1979

A126 "Ah, Those Were the Days." The New York Times (December 28, 1979).

Campbell and Alex joined their mother at Fraunces Tavern for an after-Christmas dinner for twenty-two residents of the Actors' Fund Home. Ninety-six-year old Joe Smith of the famous Smith & Dale team was in attendance.

1980

A127 Bird, David and Laurie Johnston. "Notes on People: A Reprise of the Good Old Days in the Theater." The New York Times (December 31, 1980).

At the second annual Actors' Fund holiday celebration honoring the retired actors who live at the fund's home in Englewood, N.J., Dewhurst said she would not have missed the party for anything. Twenty-five years ago when she was earning $25 a week and needed $700 for dentistry, the fund took care of the entire bill.

A128 Freeman, Don. "TV Previews." The San Diego Union (January 21, 1980).

Dewhurst is starring in Death Penalty on NBC-TV. Her career has been devoted to the stage, but lately she has turned her eyes to Hollywood for the money.

A129 Roura, Phil and Tom Poster. "People: Taking Center Stage for a Night." Daily News (December 31, 1980).

Dewhurst and her two sons attended the annual party at Fraunces Tavern for the Actors' Fund Home residents. Thirty retired performers attended the party. Joe Smith was not well enough to make it this year.

1981

A130 "Colleen Dewhurst." The New York Times (September 4, 1981).

Dewhurst is planning to go on tour next year in a new one-woman play based on the life of Carlotta Monterey, the woman Eugene O'Neill called his "wife, mistress, mother, nurse."

A131 Kakutani, Michiko. "What Makes an Actor Choose a Certain Role?" The New York Times (February 8, 1981).

Many stage actors have gone to movies and television. Hollywood is the means of financing a stage career. Actors appear on the stage for love, not money, says Dewhurst.

A132 Klemesrud, Judy. "Women Discuss Power and How to Use It." The New York Times (July 3, 1981).

In a panel discussion on "Women and the Arts," which took place at an all day session called "Women and Power" at the Sheraton Centre in New York City, Dewhurst cautioned women that their gains would be destroyed if they emulated the "absolute unfeeling, driving ambition" witnessed on the other side of the desk.

A133 Lawson, Carol. "Broadway: Coast Directors Coming East to Stage Plays." The New York Times (September 11, 1981).

Dewhurst will arrive next week on Broadway to direct Ned and Jack at the Little Theatre. The original production was staged at the Hudson Guild Theatre last season.

A134 -------------. "News of the Theater: New Role for Miss Dewhurst: Director." The New York Times (April 22, 1981).

Dewhurst makes her directing debut with Ned and Jack, a new work by Sheldon Rosen. The play opens on May 13 for a month-long run at the Hudson Guild Theatre.

A135 "26 from Broadway Voted into Theatre Hall of Fame." The New York Times (March 3, 1981).

Dewhurst has been elected to the Theatre Hall of Fame at the Gershwin Theatre in recognition of her outstanding contribution to the theatre.

1982

A136 Chadwick, Bruce. "Colleen Takes Her Act onto the Stage."
      Daily News (September 26, 1982).

      The Queen and the Rebels, a political drama, is the first Broadway
      play for the actress in four years. In between films, Dewhurst has
      also been busy as a frequent spokesman for causes: the Save The
      Theatres Committee, Pro-Choice, ERA, the Nuclear Freeze
      Movement. The actress gives her insight on the play. She
      discusses the power of television outside the New York area.

A137 Corry, John. "A New Test for Colleen Dewhurst." The New
      York Times (September 26, 1982).

      Dewhurst opens at the Plymouth in Ugo Betti's The Queen and the
      Rebels. She plays a woman whose humanity is tested in a violent
      revolution. "I like the character," she says. "She's a survivor."

A138 Kissel, Howard. "Arts & People: Dewhurst's Commitment Is Not
      Misbegotten." Women's Wear Daily (January 27, 1982).

      Dewhurst takes a weekly trip from the tranquil, wooded area of the
      upper reaches of Westchester County to the Times Square area of
      New York, where she attends the executive board meetings of the
      Actors' Fund. She discusses the importance of the Fund, which is
      sponsoring the Night of 100 Stars in February. Proceeds of the
      event will go directly to the Fund.

1983

A139 "Governor's Lady Honored by Women." Daily News (February 19,
      1983).

      At a reception in her honor tendered by the Number One Ladies
      Committee at the Sheraton Centre, Matilda Cuomo accepted a
      heart-shaped piece of Steuben glass from Dewhurst.

A140   Larkin, Kathy. " A Grand Old-Style Party." Daily News (April 7, 1983).

At the cast party for the 1983 production of You Can't Take It with You, Dewhurst said cheerfully that she was having the "best time" with the play, which was filled with fun and laughter.

A141   Sweeney, Louise. "Colleen Dewhurst: America's 'Mother Courage' Now Leaves Them Laughing." The Christian Science Monitor (May 12, 1983).

Interviewed in her apartment-hotel room in Washington, D.C. during pre-Broadway tryouts for You Can't Take It with You, Dewhurst, says it's refreshing to be playing a comic role. She is a little ill at ease, however, at the star billing for her cameo role in the third act.

1984

A142   Bennetts, Leslie. "Dewhurst Adapts to Language of Deaf Theatre." The New York Times (August 20, 1984).

Dewhurst, who has been connected with The National Theatre of the Deaf for a number of years, is directing their production of Tad Mosel's All the Way Home. She is impressed by the talent of the deaf troupe. The play will tour throughout the West, Southwest, and California during the Fall and the Northeast, Midwest, and South during the Spring of '85.

A143   Gottlieb, Martin. "Times Square Hearing Draws Array of Views." The New York Times (March 27, 1984).

As vice chairman of Save the Theatres, a theatre preservation organization, Dewhurst said that members supported the aims of the redevelopment project of the 42nd Street area. Nonetheless, they fear its success will raise land values, causing theatre owners to sell out to office developers.

1985

A144   Barthelmess, Hellen Stuart. "A Slice of Life according to Colleen Dewhurst." Westport News (July 25, 1985).

The actress summed up her new play, <u>Real Estate</u>, which was completing its run at the Westport Country Playhouse, stating "it's a dangerous play to do in summer stock . . . not your usual . . . song and dance."

A145 Dewhurst Gets O'Neill Medal." <u>The New York Times</u> (November 5, 1985).

Dewhurst was awarded the Eugene O'Neill Birthday Medal "for enriching the universal understanding" of the Nobel Prize-winning playwright. Joseph Papp, on behalf of the Theatre Committee for Eugene O'Neill, made the presentation.

1986

A146 Gardella, Kay. "Colleen Dewhurst: At 50-Plus, She's Still Waiting for a 'Dry Spell.' " <u>Daily News</u> (March 9, 1986).

Dewhurst talks about her television roles and, in particular, her rapport with Farrah Fawcett in ABC's <u>Between Two Women</u>. Dewhurst would love to work with her ex-husband again. "I told George I'd even buy tickets."

A147 Winer, Laurie. "The <u>New York Newsday</u> Interview with Colleen Dewhurst: At Ease with the Ghosts of Broadway." <u>New York Newsday</u> (August 18, 1986).

The unofficial spokesman for the fight to save the Morosco and the Helen Hayes theatres says its ironic that the view from her Actors Equity office is the Marriott Marquis Hotel. The structure darkens the streets on either side. It's as if the protests hadn't happened, and this disastrous mistake was made.

1987

A148 Dudar, Helen. "Theater: Colleen Dewhurst Portrays O'Neill's Haunted Widow." <u>The New York Times</u> (January 25, 1987).

Dewhurst plays Carlotta Monterey, the widow of Eugene O'Neill, in <u>My, Gene</u> at the Public Theater. Carlotta outlived her husband by seventeen years, the last of them as senile dementia eroded her mind and memory. Without logical dramatic continuum or fellow actors to give cues, Dewhurst finds the monodrama extremely taxing.

1988

A149 "Just Another Night with Kin." Daily News (June 16, 1988).

Long Day's Journey Into Night is a family affair both on and off stage. Dewhurst is the stage and real-life mother of cast member Campbell Scott. Alexander Scott is also involved in the production as top aide to producer Ken Marsolais, Dewhurst's long time companion.

A150 Maychick, Diana. "On the Town: Double Duty on O'Neill." New York Post (June 13, 1988).

In celebration of O'Neill's 100th anniversary, Dewhurst will tackle the light and dark sides of the poet's psyche on alternate nights in repertory. She teams with Jason Robards in both Ah, Wilderness! and Long Day's Journey and with her son Campbell Scott in the comedy.

1991

A151 Cerone, Daniel. "Murphy Brown's Farewell to Colleen Dewhurst." Los Angeles Times (October 14, 1991).

To resolve the issue of the death of Dewhurst, who appeared in the television series Murphy Brown, the writers of the show have decided to have her character die as well.

A152 "Colleen Dewhurst." Variety (August 26, 1991).

The obituary recalls the important events in the career of Dewhurst.

A153 Collins, Glenn. "Friends and Colleagues Honor Colleen Dewhurst." The New York Times (September 24, 1991).

Jason Robards read Oliver Wendell Holmes's "Chambered Nautilus." The speakers at the memorial service recalled Dewhurst's imposing presence, her distinctive, throaty voice, and her considerable personal force.

A154 La Rue, Michele. "Dewhurst's Remembrance:" Laughing through Tears." Backstage (September 27, 1991): 1, 6.

Dewhurst's own laughter set the tone of the memorial service held at the Martin Beck Theatre. Invoked by her associates on stage, it was echoed on film during the closing moments.

A155 Lipton, Lauren. "Dewhurst Wins Emmy for Murphy." Los Angeles Times (August 26, 1991).

For an appearance on Murphy Brown Dewhurst posthumously received an Emmy as outstanding guest actress in a comedy series for an appearance on Murphy Brown. The ceremony took place on August 24.

A156 Robards, Jason. "You Can Learn the Lines, But Then There Is the Mystery." The New York Times (September 1, 1991).

Robards pays a final tribute to the beautiful woman he met forty-five years ago in the Green Room of the American Academy of Dramatic Arts: "Her love was for the theatre as well as for the downtrodden and the misbegotten."

A157 Rothstein, Mervyn. "Colleen Dewhurst, the Actress, Dies at 67." The New York Times (August 24, 1991).

The obituary recalls the career of the bringer of passion and a throaty voice to the plays of O'Neill; and the president of Actors' Equity, champion of theatre causes.

A158 "Tribute Time." Women's Wear Daily (May 2, 1991).

Dewhurst was awarded the Susan Stein Shiva theatre award at a gala held at the New York Shakespeare Festival's Public Theater. Mayor David Dinkins spoke, Betty Buckley performed a Cole

Porter medley, and Jackie Mason broke up the audience: "I wanted to pay tribute to Colleen, even though she's never done a thing for me."

A159 Witchel, Alex. "For Dewhurst, an Award." The New York Times (April 19, 1991).

Colleen Dewhurst was presented the Susan Stein Shiva Award in recognition of a life in the theatre. Joseph Papp officiated.

Appendix:
Theatre and
Television Awards

1956   Village Voice Off-Broadway Obie Award. Best Actress, for her portrayal of Katharine in Shakespeare's The Taming of the Shrew and for her portrayal of the Queen in Jean Cocteau's The Eagle Has Two Heads.

1961   Antoinette Perry "Tony" Award, Best Featured Actress in a Play, for her portrayal of Mary Follet in Tad Mosel's All the Way Home.

1963   Village Voice Off-Broadway Obie Award. Best Actress, for her portrayal of Abbie Putnam in O'Neill's Desire Under the Elms.

1969   Drama Desk Vernon Rice Award. Outstanding Performance for her portrayal of Hester in Athol Fugard's Hello and Goodbye.

1974   Antoinette Perry "Tony" Award, Best Featured Actress in a Play, for her portrayal of Josie in O'Neill's A Moon for the Misbegotten.

         Drama Desk Vernon Rice Award. Outstanding Performance for her portrayal of Josie in O'Neill's A Moon for the Misbegotten.

1986   Television Emmy Award. Best Supporting Actress in a Miniseries or Special, for her role of Barbara Petherton in a miniseries, Between Two Women.

1989   Television Emmy Award. Outstanding Guest Actress in a Comedy Series, for her role as Candice Bergen's mother, <u>Murphy Brown</u>.

1989   Television Emmy Award. Best Supporting Actress in a Miniseries or Special, for her role as Margaret Page in a special <u>Those She Left Behind</u>.

1991   Television Emmy Award. Guest Actress in a comedy series, <u>Murphy Brown</u>.

Index

About the Author

BARBARA LEE HORN is Assistant Professor in the Department of Speech, Communication Sciences, and Theatre at St. John's University, Jamaica, New York. She is the author of *The Age of Hair: Evolution and Impact of Broadway's First Rock Musical* (Greenwood Press, 1991) and two previous volumes in Greenwood's series Bio-Bibliographies in the Performing Arts, *Joseph Papp: A Bio-Bibliography* (1992) and *David Merrick: A Bio-Bibliography* (1992).

Titles in
Bio-Bibliographies in the Performing Arts

Irene Dunne: A Bio-Bibliography
Margie Schultz

Anne Baxter: A Bio-Bibliography
Karin J. Fowler

Tallulah Bankhead: A Bio-Bibliography
Jeffrey L. Carrier

Jessica Tandy: A Bio-Bibliography
Milly S. Barranger

Janet Gaynor: A Bio-Bibliography
Connie Billips

James Stewart: A Bio-Bibliography
Gerard Molyneaux

Joseph Papp: A Bio-Bibliography
Barbara Lee Horn

Henry Fonda: A Bio-Bibliography
Kevin Sweeney

Edwin Booth: A Bio-Bibliography
L. Terry Oggel

Ethel Merman: A Bio-Bibliography
George B. Bryan

Lauren Bacall: A Bio-Bibliography
Brenda Scott Royce

Joseph Chaikin: A Bio-Bibliography
Alex Gildzen and Dimitris Karageorgiou

Richard Burton: A Bio-Bibliography
Tyrone Steverson

Maureen Stapleton: A Bio-Bibliography
Jeannie M. Woods

David Merrick: A Bio-Bibliography
Barbara Lee Horn

Vivien Leigh: A Bio-Bibliography
Cynthia Marylee Molt

Robert Mitchum: A Bio-Bibliography
Jerry Roberts

Agnes Moorehead: A Bio-Bibliography
Lynn Kear